JOHN JASPER

JOHN JASPER

Prepared for Publication
By
HISTORIC PULISHING
San Antonio, Texas
©2017
All Rights Reserved
Edited Materials

John Jasper:

The Unmatched Negro Philosopher and Preacher

William E. Hatcher

JOHN JASPER

JOHN JASPER

JOHN JASPER

JOHN JASPER

The Unmatched Negro Philosopher and Preacher

By

WILLIAM E. HATCHER, LL. D.

LARGE PRINT EDITION

NEW YORK CHICAGO TORONTO
Fleming H. Revell Company
LONDON AND EDINBURGH

JOHN JASPER

John Jasper.

JOHN JASPER

JOHN JASPER

JOHN JASPER

CONTENTS

JOHN JASPER

INTRODUCTION

READER; stay a moment. A word with you before you begin to sample this book. We will tell you some things in advance, which may help you to decide whether it is worthwhile to read any further. These pages deal with a negro, and are not designed either to help or to hurt the negro race. They have only to do with one man. He was one of a class,--without pedigree, and really without successors, except that he was so dominant and infectious that numbers of people affected his ways and dreamed that they were one of his sort. As a fact, they were simply of another and of a baser sort.

The man in question was a negro, and if you cannot appreciate greatness in a black skin you would do well to turn your thoughts into some other channel. Moreover, he was a negro covered over with ante bellum habits and ways of doing. He lived forty years before the war and for about forty years after it. He grew wonderfully as a freeman; but he never grew away from the tastes, dialects, and manners of the bondage times. He was a man left over from the old régime and never got infected with the new order. The air of the educated negro preacher didn't set well upon him. The raw scholarship of the new "ish," as he called it, was sounding brass to him. As a fact, the new generation of negro preachers sent out by the schools drew back from this man. They branded him as an anachronism, and felt that his presence in the pulpit was a shock to religion and an offense to the ministry; and yet not one of them ever attained the celebrity or achieved the results which came to this unlettered and grievously ungrammatical son of Africa.

But do not be afraid that you are to be fooled into the fanatical camp. This story comes from the pen of a Virginian who claims no exemption from Southern prejudices and feels no call to sound the praises of the negro race. Indeed, he never intended to write what is contained within the covers of this book. It grew up spontaneously and most of the contents were written before the book was thought of.

It is, perhaps, too much to expect that the meddlers with books will take the *ipse dixit* of an unaccredited stranger. They ought not to do it: they are not asked to do it. They can go on about their business, if they prefer; but if they do, they will miss the story of the incomparable negro of the South. This is said with sobriety and after a half century spent in close observation of the negro race.

More than that, the writer of this never had any intention of bothering with this man when he first loomed up into notoriety. He got drawn in unexpectedly. He heard that there was a marvel of a man "over in Africa," a not too savoury portion of Richmond, Virginia,--and one Sunday afternoon in company with a Scot-Irishman, who was a scholar and a critic, with a strong leaning towards ridicule, he went to hear him preach. Shades of our Anglo-Saxon fathers! Did mortal lips ever gush with such

torrents of horrible English! Hardly a word came out
clothed and in its right mind. And gestures! He circled
around the pulpit with his ankle in his hand; and laughed
and sang and shouted and acted about a dozen characters
within the space of three minutes. Meanwhile, in spite of
these things, he was pouring out a gospel sermon, red hot,
full of love, full of invective, full of tenderness, full of
bitterness, full of tears, full of every passion that ever
flamed in the human breast. He was a theatre within
himself, with the stage crowded with actors. He was a
battle-field;--himself the general, the staff, the officers,
the common soldiery, the thundering artillery and the
rattling musketry. He was the preacher; likewise the
church and the choir and the deacons and the
congregation. The Scot-Irishman surrendered in fifteen
minutes after the affair commenced, but the other man
was hard-hearted and stubborn and refused to commit
himself. He preferred to wait until he got out of doors and
let the wind blow on him and see what was left. He
determined to go again; and he went and kept going, off
and on, for twenty years. That was before the negro
became a national figure. It was before he started his race
with his philosophy as to the rotation of the sun. It was
before he became a lecturer and a sensation, sought after
from all parts of the country. Then it was that he captured
the Scot-Irish and the other man also. What is written
here constitutes the gatherings of nearly a quarter of a
century, and, frankly speaking, is a tribute to the brother

in black,--the one unmatched, unapproachable, and wonderful brother.

But possibly the reader is of the practical sort. He would like to get the worldly view of this African genius and to find out of what stuff he was made. Very well; he will be gratified! Newspapers are heartlessly practical. They are grudging of editorial commendation, and in Richmond, at the period, they were sparing of references of any kind to negroes. You could hardly expect them to say anything commendatory of a negro, if he was a negro, with odd and impossible notions. Now this man was of that very sort. He got it into his big skull that the earth was flat, and that the sun rotated;--a scientific absurdity! But you see he proved it by the Bible. He ransacked the whole book and got up ever so many passages. He took them just as he found them. It never occurred to him that the Bible was not dealing with natural science, and that it was written in an age and country when astronomy was unknown and therefore written in the language of the time. Intelligent people understand this very well, but this miracle of his race was behind his era. He took the Bible literally, and, with it in hand, he fought his battles about the sun. Literally, but not scientifically, he proved his position, and he gave some of his devout antagonists a world of botheration by the tenacity with which he held to his views and the power with which he stated his case. Scientifically, he was one of the ancients, but that did not interfere with his piety and did not at all eclipse his views. His perfect honesty was most apparent in all of his contentions; and, while some laughed at what they called his vagaries, those who knew him best respected him none the less, but rather the more, for his astronomical combat. There was something in his love of the Bible, his faith in every letter of it, and his courage, that drew to him the good will and lofty respect of uncounted thousands and, probably, it might be said, of uncounted millions.

Now when this man died it was as the fall of a tower. It was a crash, heard and felt farther than was the collapse of the famous tower at Venice. If the dubious, undecided reader has not broken down on the road but has come this far, he is invited to look at the subjoined editorial from *The Richmond Dispatch*, the leading morning paper of Richmond, Va., which published at the time an article on this lofty figure, now national in its proportions and imperishable in its fame, when it bowed to the solemn edict of death.

(From *The Richmond Dispatch*)

"It is a sad coincidence that the destruction of the Jefferson Hotel and the death of the Rev. John Jasper should have fallen upon the same day. John Jasper was a Richmond Institution, as surely so as was Major Ginter's fine hotel. He was a national character, and he and his philosophy were known from one end of the land to the other. Some people have the impression that John Jasper was famous simply because he flew in the face of the scientists and declared that the sun moved. In one sense, that is true, but it is also true that his fame was due, in great measure, to a strong personality, to a deep, earnest conviction, as well as to a devout Christian character. Some preachers might have made this assertion about the sun's motion without having attracted any special attention. The people would have laughed over it, and the incident would have passed by as a summer breeze. But John Jasper made an impression upon his generation, because he was sincerely and deeply in earnest in all that he said. No man could talk with him in private, or listen to him from the pulpit, without being thoroughly convinced of that fact. His implicit trust in the Bible and everything in it, was beautiful and impressive. He had no other lamp by which his feet were guided. He had no other science, no other philosophy. He took the Bible in its literal significance; he accepted it as the inspired word of God; he trusted it with all his heart and soul and mind; he believed nothing that was in conflict with the teachings of the Bible--scientists and philosophers and theologians to the contrary notwithstanding.

" 'They tried to make it appear,' said he, in the last talk we had with him on the subject, 'that John Jasper was a fool and a liar when he said that the sun moved. I paid no attention to it at first, because I did not believe that the so-called scientists were in earnest. I did not think that there was any man in the world fool enough to believe that the sun did *not* move, for everybody had seen it move. But when I found that these so-called scientists were in earnest I took down my old Bible and proved that they, and not John Jasper, were the fools and the liars.' And there was no more doubt in his mind on that subject than there was of his existence. John Jasper had the faith that removed mountains. He knew the literal Bible as well as Bible scholars did. He did not understand it from the scientific point of view, but he knew its teachings and understood its spirit, and he believed in it. He accepted it as the true word of God, and he preached it with unction and with power.

"John Jasper became famous by accident, but he was a most interesting man apart from his solar theory. He was a man of deep convictions, a man with a purpose in life, a man who earnestly desired to save souls for heaven. He followed his divine calling with faithfulness, with a determination, as far as he could, to make the ways of his God known unto men, His saving health among all nations. And the Lord poured upon His servant, Jasper, 'the continual dew of His blessing.'"

I
JASPER PRESENTED

JOHN JASPER, the negro preacher of Richmond, Virginia, stands preëminent among the preachers of the negro race in the South. He was for fifty years a slave, and a preacher during twenty-five years of his slavery, and distinctly of the old plantation type. Freedom came full-handed to him, but it did not in any notable degree change him in his style, language, or manner of preaching. He was the ante bellum preacher until eighty-nine years of age, when he preached his last sermon on "Regeneration," and with quiet dignity laid off his mortal coil and entered the world invisible. He was the last of his type, and we shall not look upon his like again. It has been my cherished purpose for some time to embalm the memory of this extraordinary genius in some form that would preserve it from oblivion. I would give to the American people a picture of the God-made preacher who was great in his bondage and became immortal in his freedom.

This is not to be done in biographic form, but rather in vagrant articles which find their kinship only in the fact that they present some distinct view of a man, hampered by early limitations, denied the graces of culture, and cut off even from the advantages of a common education, but who was munificently endowed by nature, filled with vigour and self-reliance, and who achieved greatness in spite of almost limitless adversities. I account him genuinely great among the sons of men, but I am quite sure that the public can never apprehend the force and gist of his rare manhood without first being made acquainted with certain facts appertaining to his early life.

Jasper was born a slave. He grew up on a plantation and was a toiler in the fields up to his manhood. When he came to Richmond, now grown to a man, he was untutored, full of dangerous energies, almost gigantic in his muscle, set on pleasure, and without the fear of God before his eyes. From his own account of himself, he was fond of display, a gay coxcomb among the women of his race, a fun-maker by nature, with a self-assertion that made him a leader within the circles of his freedom.

We meet him first as one of the "hands" in the tobacco factory of Mr. Samuel Hargrove, an enterprising and prosperous manufacturer in the city of Richmond. Jasper occupied the obscure position of "a stemmer,"-- which means that his part was to take the well-cured tobacco leaf and eliminate the stem, with a view to preparing what was left to be worked into "the plug" which is the glory of the tobacco-chewer. This position had one advantage for this quick-witted and alert young slave. It threw him into contact with a multitude of his own race, and as nature had made him a lover of his kind his social qualities found ample scope for exercise. In his early days he went at a perilous pace and found in the path of the sinful many fountains of common joy. Indeed, he made evil things fearfully fascinating by the zestful and remorseless way in which he indulged them.

It was always a joy renewed for him to tell the story of his conversion. As described by him, his initial religious experiences, while awfully mystical and solemn to him, were grotesque and ludicrous enough. They partook of the extravagances of the times, yet were so honest in their nature, and so soundly Scriptural in their doctrines, and so reverential in their tone, that not even the most captious sceptic could hear him tell of them, in his moments of exalted inspiration, without feeling profoundly moved by them.

It ought to be borne in mind that this odd and forcible man was a preacher in Richmond for a half century, and that during all that time, whether in slavery or in freedom, he lived up to his religion, maintaining his integrity, defying the unscrupulous efforts of jealous foes to destroy him, and walking the high path of spotless and incorruptible honour. Not that he was always popular among his race. He was too decided, too aggressive, too intolerant towards meanness, and too unpitying in his castigation of vice, to be popular. His life, in the nature of the case, had to be a warfare, and it may be truly said that he slept with his sword buckled on.

Emancipation did not turn his head. He was the same high-minded, isolated, thoughtful Jasper. His way of preaching became an offense to the "edicated" preachers of the new order, and with their new sense of power these double-breasted, Prince-Albert-coated, high hat and kid-gloved clergymen needed telescopes to look as far down as Jasper was, to get a sight of him. They verily thought that it would be a simple process to transfix him with their sneers, and flaunt their new grandeurs before him, in order to annihilate him. Many of these new-fledged preachers, who came from the schools to be pastors in Richmond, resented Jasper's prominence and fame. They felt that he was a reproach to the race, and they did not fail to fling at him their flippant sneers.

But Jasper's mountain stood strong. He looked this new tribe of his adversaries over and marked them as a calcimined and fictitious type of culture. To him they were shop-made and unworthy of respect. They called forth the storm of his indignant wrath. He opened his batteries upon them, and, for quite a while, the thunder of his guns fairly shook the steeples on the other negro churches of Richmond. And yet it will never do to think of him as the incarnation of a vindictive and malevolent spirit. He dealt terrific blows, and it is hardly too much to say that many of his adversaries found it necessary to get out of the range of his guns. But, after all, there was a predominant good nature about him. His humour was inexhaustible, and irresistible as well. If by his fiery denunciations he made his people ready to "fight Philip," he was quite apt before he finished to let fly some of his odd comparisons, his laughable stories, or his humorous mimicries. He could laugh off his own grievances, and could make his own people "take the same medicine."

Jasper was something of a hermit, given to seclusion, imperturbably calm in his manner, quite ascetic in his tastes, and a cormorant in his devouring study of the Bible. Naturally, Jasper was as proud as Lucifer,--too proud to be egotistic and too candid and self-assertive to affect a humility which he did not feel. He walked heights where company was scarce, and seemed to love his solitude. Jasper was as brave as a lion and possibly not a little proud of his bravery. He fought in the open and set no traps for his adversaries. He believed in himself,--felt the dignity of his position, and never let himself down to what was little or unseemly.

The most remarkable fact in Jasper's history is connected with his extraordinary performances in connection with his tersely expressed theory,--THE SUN DO MOVE! We would think in advance that any man who would come forward to champion that view would be hooted out of court. It was not so with Jasper. His bearing through all that excitement was so dignified, so sincere, so consistent and heroic, that he actually did win the rank of a true philosopher. This result, so surprising, is possibly the most handsome tribute to his inherent excellence and nobility of character. One could not fail to see that his fight on a technical question was so manifestly devout, so filled with zeal for the honour of religion, and so courageous in the presence of overwhelming odds, that those who did not agree with him learned to love and honour him.

The sensation which he awakened fairly flew around the country. It is said that he preached the sermon 250 times, and it would be hard to estimate how many thousands of people heard him. The papers, religious and secular, had much to say about him. Many of them published his sermons, some of them at first plying him with derision, but about all of them rounding up with the admission of a good deal of faith in Jasper. So vast was his popularity that a mercenary syndicate once undertook to traffic on his popularity by sending him forth as a public lecturer. The movement proved weak on its feet, and after a little travel he hobbled back richer in experience than in purse.

As seen in the pulpit or in the street Jasper was an odd picture to look upon. His figure was uncouth; he was rather loosely put together; his limbs were fearfully long and his body strikingly short,--a sort of nexus to hold his head and limbs in place. He was black, but his face saved him. It was open, luminous, thoughtful, and in moments of animation it glowed with a radiance and exultation that was most attractive.

Jasper's career as a preacher after the war was a poem. The story is found later on and marks him as a man of rare originality, and of patience born of a better world. He left a church almost entirely the creation of his own productive life, that holds a high rank in Richmond and that time will find it hard to estrange from his spirit and influence. For quite a while he was hardly on coöperative terms with the neighbouring churches, and it is possible that he ought to share somewhat in the responsibility for the estrangement which so long existed;--though it might be safely said that if they had left Jasper alone he would not have bothered them. Let it be said that the animosities of those days gradually gave away to the gracious and softening influence of time, and, when his end came, all the churches and ministers of the city most cordially and lovingly united in honouring his memory.

It may betoken the regard in which Jasper was held by the white people if I should be frank enough to say that I was the pastor of the Grace Street Baptist Church, one of the largest ecclesiastical bodies in the city at the time of Jasper's death, and the simple announcement in the morning papers that I would deliver an address in honour of this negro preacher who had been carried to his grave during the previous week brought together a representative and deeply sympathetic audience which overflowed the largest church auditorium in the city. With the utmost affection and warmth I put forth my lofty appreciation of this wonderful prince of his tribe, and so far as known there was never an adverse criticism offered as to the propriety or justice of the tribute which was paid him.

JOHN JASPER

It is of this unusual man, this prodigy of his race, and this eminent type of the Christian negro, that the somewhat random articles of this volume are to treat. His life jumped the common grooves and ran on heights not often trod. His life went by bounds and gave surprises with each succeeding leap.

II
JASPER HAS A THRILLING CONVERSION

LET us bear in mind that at the time of his conversion John Jasper was a slave, illiterate and working in a tobacco factory in Richmond. It need hardly be said that he shared the superstitions and indulged in the extravagances of his race, and these in many cases have been so blatant and unreasonable that they have caused some to doubt the negro's capacity for true religion. But from the beginning Jasper's religious experiences showed forth the Lord Jesus as their source and centre. His thoughts went to the Cross. His hope was founded on the sacrificial blood, and his noisy and rhapsodic demonstrations sounded a distinct note in honour of his Redeemer.

Jasper's conviction as to his call to the ministry was clear-cut and intense. He believed that his call came straight from God. His boast and glory was that he was a God-made preacher. In his fierce warfares with the educated preachers of his race,--"the new issue," as he contemptuously called them--he rested his claim on the ground that God had put him into the ministry; and so reverential, so full of noble assertion and so irresistibly eloquent was he in setting forth his ministerial authority that even his most sceptical critics were constrained to admit that, like John the Baptist, he was "a man sent from God."

And yet Jasper knew the human side of his call. It was a part of his greatness that he could see truth in its relations and completeness, and while often he presented one side of a truth, as if it were all of it, he also saw the other side. With him a paradox was not a contradiction. He gratefully recognized the human influences which helped him to enter the ministry. While preaching one Sunday afternoon Jasper suddenly stopped, his face lighted as with a vision, a rich laugh rippled from his lips while his eyes flashed with soulful fire. He then said, in a manner never to be reported: "Mars Sam Hargrove called me to preach de Gospel--he was my old marster, and he started me out wid my message." Instantly the audience quivered with quickened attention, for they knew at once that the man in the pulpit had something great to tell.

"I was seekin' God six long weeks--jes' 'cause I was sich a fool I couldn't see de way De Lord struck me fus' on Cap'tal Squar', an' I left thar badly crippled. One July mornin' somethin' happen'd. I was a tobarker-stemmer-- dat is, I took de tobarker leaf, an' tor'd de stem out, an' dey won't no one in dat fac'ry

could beat me at dat work. But dat mornin' de stems wouldn't come out to save me, an' I tor'd up tobarker by de poun' an' flung it under de table. Fac' is, bruthr'n, de darkness of death was in my soul dat mornin'. My sins was piled on me like mount'ns; my feet was sinkin' down to de reguns of despar, an' I felt dat of all sinners I was de wust. I tho't dat I would die right den, an' wid what I supposed was my lars breath I flung up to heav'n a cry for mercy. 'Fore I kno'd it, de light broke; I was light as a feather; my feet was on de mount'n; salvation rol'd like a flood thru my soul, an' I felt as if I could 'nock off de fact'ry roof wid my shouts.

"But I sez to mysef, I gwine to hol' still till dinner, an' so I cried, an' laffed, an' tore up de tobarker. Pres'ntly I looked up de table, an' dar was a old man--he luv me, an' tried hard to lead me out de darkness, an' I slip roun' to whar he was, an' I sez in his ear as low as I could: 'Hallelujah; my soul is redeemed!' Den I jump back quick to my work, but after I once open my mouf it was hard to keep it shet any mo'. 'Twan' long 'fore I looked up de line agin, an' dar was a good ol' woman dar dat knew all my sorrers, an' had been prayin' fur me all de time. Der was no use er talkin'; I had to tell her, an' so I skip along up quiet as a breeze, an' start'd to whisper in her ear, but just den de holin-back straps of Jasper's breachin' broke, an' what I tho't would be a whisper was loud enuf to be hearn clean 'cross Jeems River to Manchester. One man sed he tho't de factory was fallin' down; all I know'd I had raise my fust shout to de glory of my Redeemer.

"But for one thing thar would er been a jin'ral revival in de fact'ry dat mornin'. Dat one thing was de overseer. He bulg'd into de room, an' wid a voice dat sounded like he had his breakfus dat mornin' on rasps an' files, bellowed out: 'What's all dis row 'bout?' Somebody shouted out dat John Jasper dun got religun, but dat didn't wurk 'tall wid de boss. He tell me to git back to my table, an' as he had sumpthin' in his hand dat looked ugly, it was no time fur makin' fine pints, so I sed: 'Yes, sir, I will; I ain't meant no harm; de fus taste of salvation got de better un me, but I'll git back to my work.' An' I tell you I got back quick.

"Bout dat time Mars Sam he come out'n his orfis, an' he say: 'What's de matter out here?' An' I hear de overseer tellin' him: 'John Jasper kick up a fuss, an' say he dun got religun, but I dun fix him, an' he got back to his table.' De devil tol' me to hate de overseer dat mornin', but de luv of God was rollin' thru my soul, an' somehow I didn't mind what he sed.

"Little aft'r I hear Mars Sam tell de overseer he want to see Jasper. Mars Sam was a good man; he was a Baptis', an' one of de hed men of de old Fust Church down here, an' I was glad when I hear Mars Sam say he want to see me. When I git in his orfis, he say: 'John, what was de matter out dar jes' now?'--and his voice was sof' like, an' it seem'd to have a little song in it which play'd into my soul like an angel's harp. I sez to him: 'Mars Sam, ever sence de fourth of July I ben cryin' after de Lord, six long weeks, an' jes' now out dar at de table God tuk my sins away, an' set my feet on a rock. I didn't mean to make no noise, Mars Sam, but 'fore I know'd it de fires broke out in my soul, an' I jes' let go one shout to de glory of my Saviour.'

"Mars Sam was settin' wid his eyes a little down to de flo', an' wid a pritty quiv'r in his voice he say very slo': 'John, I b'leve dat way myself. I luv de Saviour dat you have jes' foun', an' I wan' to tell you dat I do'n complain 'cause you made de noise jes' now as you did.' Den Mars Sam did er thing dat nearly made me drop to de flo'. He git out of his chair, an' walk over to me and giv' me his han', and he say: 'John, I wish you mighty well. Your Saviour is mine, an' we are bruthers in de Lord.' When he say dat, I turn 'round an' put my arm agin de wall, an' held my mouf to keep from shoutin'. Mars Sam well know de good he dun me.

"Art'r awhile he say: 'John, did you tell eny of 'em in thar 'bout your conversion?' And I say: 'Yes, Mars Sam, I tell 'em fore I kno'd it, an' I feel like tellin' eberybody in de worl' about it.' Den he say: 'John, you may tell it. Go back in dar an' go up an' down de tables, an' tell all of 'em. An' den if you wan' to, go up-stars an' tell 'em all 'bout it, an' den down-stars an' tell de hogshed men an' de drivers an' everybody what de Lord has dun for yor.'

"By dis time Mars Sam's face was rainin' tears, an' he say: 'John, you needn' work no mo' today. I giv' you holiday. Aft'r you git thru tellin' it here at de fact'ry, go up to de house, an' tell your folks; go roun' to your neighbours, an' tell dem; go enywhere you wan' to, an' tell de good news. It'll do you good, do dem good, an' help to hon'r your Lord an' Saviour.'

"Oh, dat happy day! Can I ever forgit it? Dat was my conversion mornin', an' dat day de Lord sent me out wid de good news of de kingdom. For mo' den forty years I've ben tellin' de story. My step is gittin' ruther slo', my voice breaks down, an' sometimes I am awful tired, but still I'm tellin' it. My lips shall proclaim de dyin' luv of de Lam' wid my las' expirin' breath.

"Ah, my dear ol' marster! He sleeps out yonder in de ol' cemetery, an' in dis worl' I shall see his face no mo', but I don't forgit him. He give me a holiday, an' sent me out to tell my friends what great things God had dun for my soul. Oft'n as I preach I feel that I'm doin' what my ol' marster tol' me to do. If he was here now, I think he would lif' up dem kin' black eyes of his, an' say: 'Dat's right, John; still tellin' it; fly like de angel, an' wherever you go carry de Gospel to de people.' Farewell, my ol' marster, when I lan' in de heav'nly city, I'll call at your mansion dat de Lord had ready for you when you got dar, an' I shall say: 'Mars Sam, I did what you tol' me, an' many of 'em is comin' up here wid da robes wash'd in de blood of de Lam' dat was led into de way by my preachin', an' as you started me I want you to shar' in de glory of da salvation. 'An' I tell you what I reek'n, dat when Mars Sam sees me, he'll say: 'John, call me marster no mo'; we're bruthers now, an' we'll live forever roun' de throne of God.' "

This is Jasper's story, but largely in his own broken words. When he told it, it swept over the great crowd like a celestial gale. The people seemed fascinated and transfigured. His homely way of putting the Gospel came home to them. Let me add that his allusions to his old master were in keeping with his kindly and conciliatory tone in all that he had to say about the white people after the emancipation of the slaves. He loved the white people, and among them his friends and lovers were counted by the thousand.

III
HOW JASPER GOT HIS SCHOOLING

THESE chapters disclaim outright any pretension to biography. They deal with a weird, indescribable and mysterious genius, standing out in gloomy grandeur, and not needing the setting forth of ordinary incidents. At the same time, when an extraordinary man comes along and does masterful things, there be some who are ready to ask questions. Was he educated? Well, yes, he was. He had rare educational advantages, not in the schools; but what of that? A genius has no use for a school, except so far as it teaches him the art of thinking. If we run back to the boyhood of Jasper and look him over we find that he had, after all, distinct educational advantages.

It is another case of a good mother. We know that her name was Nina, and that she was the wife of Philip Jasper, and if tradition tells the truth she was the mother of twenty-four children--a premature applicant for the Rooseveltian prize. John was the last, and was not born until two months after his father's death. Truly grace as well as genius was needed in his case, or he would have struck the wrong road.

That mother was the head of the working women on the Fluvanna farm and learned to govern by reason of the position she held. Her appointment bespoke her character, and her work improved it. Later on, she became in another home the chief of the servant force in a rich family. It was quite a good place. It brought her in contact with cultivated people and the imitative quality in the negro helped her to learn the manners and to imbibe the spirit of the lady. Later on still, she became a nurse to look after the sick at the Negro Quarters. There she had to do with doctors, medicines and counsellors and helpers. Add to all this, she was a sober, thoughtful, godly woman, and you will quite soon reach the conclusion that she was a very excellent teacher for John; and John coming latest in the domestic procession found her rich in experience, matured in motherliness, and enlarged in her outlook of life.

John's father was a preacher. Harsh things, and some of them needlessly false, are said of the fact that there were no negro preachers in the times of the slaveholding. It is true, that the laws of the country did not allow independent organizations of negroes, and negro preachers were not allowed, except by the consent of their masters, to go abroad preaching the Gospel. They could not accept pastoral charges, and were hampered, as all must admit, by grievous restrictions, but there were negro preachers in that day just the same,--scores of them, and in one way and another they had many privileges and did good and effective service. One thing about the negro preacher of the ante bellum era was his high character. It is true that the owner of slaves was not in all cases adapted to determine the moral character of the slave who wanted to preach, and too often, it may be admitted, his prejudices and self-interest may have ruled out some men who ought to have been allowed to preach. It is a pity if this were true. But this strictness had one advantage. When the master of a negro man allowed him to preach it was an endorsement, acceptable and satisfactory, wherever the man went. If they thought he was all right at home, he could pass muster elsewhere.

Now, concerning John's father, tradition has proved exceedingly partial. It has glorified Tina the mother with fine extravagance, but it has cut Philip unmercifully. John could get little out of his father, for they were not contemporaries, and as his brothers and sisters seemed to have been born for oblivion, we can trace little of his distinction to the old household in Fluvanna.

But we dare say that Philip, the preacher, remembered chiefly because he was a preacher, had something to do in a subtle way with John's training. Nor must we fail to remember that Jasper himself grew up in contact with a fine old Virginia family. Fools there be many who love to talk of the shattering of the old aristocracy of Virginia. The "F.F.V.'s"[1] have been the sport of the vulgar, and their downfall has been a tragedy which the envious greedily turned into a comedy. But people ought to have some sense. They ought to see things in their proper relation. They ought to know that in the atmosphere of the old Virginia home the negroes, and especially those who served in person the heads of the family, caught the cue of the gentleman and the lady. I can stand on the streets of Richmond to-day and pick out the coloured men and women who grew up in homes of refinement, and who still bear about them the signs of it. Bent by age, and many of them tortured by infirmity, they still bear the marks of their old masters. They constitute a class quite apart from those of later times and are unequalled by them. I rejoice in all the comforts and advantages which have come to the negroes,--most heartily I thank heaven for their freedom and for all that freedom has brought them; but I do not hesitate to say that one of the losses was that contact with courtly, dignified, and royal people which many of them had before the Civil War. And even those on the plantations, while removed farther from the lights of the great castles in which their masters lived, walked not in darkness entirely, but unconsciously felt the transforming power of those times.

1 First Families of Virginia

John Jasper was himself an aristocrat. His mode of dress, his manner of walking, his lofty dignity, all told the story. He received an aristocratic education, and he never lost it. Besides this, he had a most varied experience as a slave. He grew up on the farm, and knew what it was to be a plantation hand. He learned to work in the tobacco factory. He worked also in the foundries, and also served around the houses of the families with whom he lived; for it must be understood that after the breaking up of the

Peachy family he changed owners and lived in different places. These things enlarged his scope, and with that keen desire to know things he learned at every turn of life.

After his conversion he became a passionate student. He acknowledges one who sought to teach him to read, and after he became a preacher he spelled out the Bible for himself. He was eager to hear other men preach and to talk with those who were wiser than he. And so he kept on learning as long as he lived, though of course he missed the help of the schools, and never crossed the threshold of worldly science in his pursuit of knowledge.

It may be well to say here that Jasper never lost his pride in white people. He delighted to be with them. Thousands upon thousands went to hear him, and while there was a strain of curiosity in many of them there was an under-note of respect and kindliness which always thrilled his heart and did him good. Time and again he spoke to me personally of white people, and always with a beautiful appreciation. It is noteworthy that the old man rode his high horse when his house was partly filled with white people, and it would be no exaggeration to say that not since the end of the war has any negro been so much loved or so thoroughly believed in as John Jasper.

IV
THE SLAVE PREACHER

IT is as a preacher that John Jasper is most interesting. His personality was notable and full of force anywhere, but the pulpit was the stage of his chief performance. It is worthwhile to bear in mind that he began to preach in 1839 and that was twenty-five years before the coming of freedom. For a quarter of a century, therefore, he was a preacher while yet a slave. His time, of course, under the law belonged to his master, and under the laws of the period, he could preach only under very serious limitations. He could go only when his master said he might, and he could preach only when some white minister or committee was present to see that things were conducted in an orderly way. This is the hard way of stating the case, but there are many ways of getting around such regulations. The man who could preach, though a negro, rarely failed of an opportunity to preach. The man who was fit for the work had friends who enabled him to "shy around" his limitations.

There was one thing which the negro greatly insisted upon, and which not even the most hard-hearted masters were ever quite willing to deny them. They could never bear that their dead should be put away without a funeral. Not that they expected, at the time of the burial, to have the funeral service. Indeed, they did not desire it, and it was never according to their notions. A funeral to them was a pageant. It was a thing to be arranged for a long time ahead. It was to be marked by the gathering of the kindred and friends from far and wide. It was not satisfactory unless there was a vast and excitable crowd. It usually meant an all-day meeting, and often a meeting in a grove, and it drew white and black alike, sometimes almost in equal numbers. Another demand in the case,-- for the slaves knew how to make their demands,--was that the negro preacher "should preach the funeral," as they called it. In things like this, the wishes of the slaves generally prevailed. "The funeral" loomed up weeks in advance, and although marked by sable garments, mournful manners and sorrowful outcries, it had about it hints of an elaborate social function with festive accompaniments. There was much staked on the fame of the officiating brother. He must be one of their own colour, and a man of reputation. They must have a man to plough up their emotional depths, and they must have freedom to indulge in the extravagancies of their sorrow. These demonstrations were their tribute to their dead and were expected to be fully adequate to do honour to the family.

It was in this way that Jasper's fame began. At first, his tempestuous, ungrammatical eloquence was restricted to Richmond, and there it was hedged in with many humbling limitations. But gradually the news concerning this fiery and thrilling orator sifted itself into the country, and many invitations came for him to officiate at country funerals.

He was preëminently a funeral preacher. A negro funeral without an uproar, without shouts and groans, without fainting women and shouting men, without pictures of triumphant deathbeds and the judgment day, and without the gates of heaven wide open and the subjects of the funeral dressed in white and rejoicing around the throne of the Lamb, was no funeral at all. Jasper was a master from the outset at this work. One of his favourite texts, as a young preacher, was that which was recorded in Revelations, sixth chapter, and second verse: "And I saw and beheld a white horse; and he that sat upon him had a bow, and a crown was given unto him, and he went forth conquering and to conquer." Before the torrent of his florid and spectacular eloquence the people were swept down to the ground, and sometimes for hours many seemed to be in trances, not a few lying as if they were dead.

Jasper's first visit to the country as a preacher of which we have any account was to Hanover County. A prominent and wealthy slaveholder had the custom of allowing his servants to have imposing funerals, when their kindred and friends died; but those services were always conducted by a white minister. In some way the fame of Jasper had penetrated that community, and one of the slaves asked his master to let Jasper come and attend the funeral. But to this the master made an objection. He knew nothing about Jasper, and did not believe that any negro was capable of preaching the Gospel with good effect. This negro was not discouraged by the refusal of the proprietor of the great plantation to grant his request. He went out and collected a number of most trustworthy and influential negro men and they came in a body to his master and renewed the plea. They told him in their way about what a great man Jasper was, how anxious they were to hear him, what a comfort his presence would be to the afflicted family, and how thankful they would be to have their request honoured. They won their point in part. He said to them, as if yielding reluctantly, "very well, let him come." They however had something more to say. They knew Jasper would need to have a good reason in order to get his master's consent for him to come, and they knew that Jasper would not come unless he came under the invitation and protection of the white people, and therefore they asked the gentleman if he would not write a letter inviting him to come. Accordingly, in a spirit of compromise and courtesy very pleasing to the coloured people, the letter was written and Jasper came.

The news of his expected coming spread like a flame. Not only the country people in large numbers, but quite a few of the Richmond people, made ready to attend the great occasion. Jasper went out in a private conveyance, the distance not being great, and, in his kind wish to take along as many friends as possible, he overloaded the wagon and had a breakdown. The delay in his arrival was very long and unexplained; but still the people lingered and beguiled the time with informal religious services.

At length the Richmond celebrity appeared on the scene late in the day. The desire to hear him was imperative, and John Jasper was equal to the occasion. Late as the hour was, and wearied as were the people, he spoke with overmastering power. The owner of the great company of slaves on that plantation was among his hearers, and he could not resist the spell of devout eloquence which poured from the lips of the unscholared Jasper. It was a sermon from the heart, full of personal passion and hot with gospel fervour, and the heart of the lord of the plantation was powerfully moved. He undertook to engage Jasper to preach on the succeeding Sunday and handed the blushing preacher quite a substantial monetary token of his appreciation.

The day was accounted memorable by reason of the impression which Jasper made. Indeed, Jasper was a master of assemblies. No politician could handle a crowd with more consummate tact than he. He was the king of hearts and could sway throngs as the wind shakes the trees.

There is a facetious story abroad among the negroes that in those days Jasper went to Farmville to officiate on a funeral occasion where quite a number of the dead were to have their virtues commemorated and where their "mouming friends," as Jasper in time came to call them, were to be comforted. The news that Jasper was to be there went out on the wings of the wind and vast throngs attended. Of course, a white minister was present and understood that he was the master of ceremonies. The story is, that he felt that it would not be safe to entrust an occasion so vastly interesting to the hands of Jasper, and he decided that he would quiet Jasper and satisfy the public demands by calling on Jasper to pray. As a fact, Jasper was about as much of an orator in speaking to heaven as he was in speaking to mortal men. His prayer had such contagious and irresistible eloquence that whatever the Lord did about it, it surely brought quite a resistless response from the crowd. When the white preacher ended his tame and sapless address, the multitude cried out for Jasper. Inspired by the occasion and emboldened by the evident disposition to shut him out, Jasper took fire and on eagle wings he mounted into the heavens and gave such a brilliant and captivating address that the vast crowd went wild with joy and enthusiasm

There is yet another story of a time when Jasper was called into the country where he and a white minister were to take part in one of the combined funerals so common at that time. Upon arriving at the church the white minister was unutterably shocked to find that his associate in the services was a negro. That was too much for him, and he decided on the spot that if he went in, Jasper would have to stay out, and he decided that he would go in and would stay in until the time was over and leave Jasper to his reflections on the outside. For two hours the white brother beat the air, killed time, and quite wearied the crowd by his lumbering and tiresome discourse. After he had arrived at the point where it seemed that no more could be said, the exhausted and exhausting brother closed his sermon and was arranging to end the service. But the people would not have it so. Tumultuously they cried out for Jasper,--a cry in which the whites outdid the blacks. It was not in Jasper to ignore such appreciation. Of all men, he had the least desire or idea of being snubbed or side-tracked. With that mischievous smile which was born of the jubilant courage of his soul, Jasper came forth. He knew well the boundaries of his rights, and needed no danger signals to warn him off hostile ground. For fifteen or twenty minutes he poured forth a torrent of passionate oratory,-- not empty and frivolous words, but a message rich with comfort and help, and uttered only as he could utter it. The effect was electrical. The white people crowded around him to congratulate and thank him, and went away telling the story of his greatness.

Tradition has failed to give us the name of the ill-fated brother who in seeking to kill time, seemed to have got knocked into oblivion. It is worth while to say that the white ministers were within the law in attending occasions like those described above and felt the necessity of care and discretion in managing the exercises, lest the hostilities of irreligious people should be excited against the negroes. It is due to the white people, and especially to that denomination to which John Jasper was associated, to say that under their influence the negroes, who were practically barbarians when they were brought into the South, were civilized and Christianized. A large proportion of them were well-mannered and nobly-behaved Christians at the time their slavery ended. The church buildings were always constructed so that the white people and the negroes could worship in the same house. They were baptized by the same minister, they sat down together at the communion table, they heard the same sermons, sang the same songs, were converted at the same meetings, and were baptized at the same time. Ofttimes, and in almost all places, they were allowed to have services to themselves. In this, of course, they enjoyed a larger freedom than when they met in the same house with the white people.

They know little of the facts who imagine that there was estrangement and alienation between the negroes and the whites in the matter of religion. Far from it. There was much of good fellowship between the whites and negroes in the churches, and the white ministers took notable interest in the religious welfare of the slaves. They often visited them pastorally and gladly talked with them about their salvation. These chapters are not intended either to defend or to condemn slavery; but in picturing the condition of things which encompassed Jasper during the days of slavery, it is worth while to let it be understood that it was during their bondage and under the Christian influence of Southern people, that the negroes of the South were made a Christian people. It was the best piece of missionary work ever yet done upon the face of the earth.

Another fact should be referred to here. Jasper was a pastor in the City of Petersburg even before the breaking out of the Civil War. He had charge of one of the less prominent negro churches and went over from Richmond for two Sundays in each month. This, of course, showed the enlargement of his liberty, that he could take the time to leave the city so often in pursuance of his ministerial work.

It need hardly be mentioned that his presence in Petersburg brought unusual agitation. He fairly depopulated the other negro churches and drew crowds that could not be accommodated. When it was rumoured that Jasper was to preach for the first time on Sunday afternoon, the Rev. Dr. Keene, of the First Baptist Church, and many other white people attended. They were much concerned lest his coming should produce a disturbance, and they went with the idea of preventing any undue excitement. Jasper, flaming with fervid zeal and exhilarated with the freedom of the truth, carried everything before him. He had not preached long before the critical white people were stirred to the depths of their souls and their emotion showed in their weeping.

They beheld and felt the wonderful power of the man. It is said that Dr. Keene was completely captivated, and recognized in Jasper a man whom God had called.

V
"WHAR SIN KUM FRUM?"

My first sight of Jasper must always remain in the chapter of unforgotten things. The occasion was Sunday afternoon, and the crowd was overflowing. Let me add that it was one of his days of spiritual intoxication, and he played on every key in the gamut of the human soul.

Two questions had been shot at him, and they both took effect. The first had to do with creation. For a half hour he pounded away on the creatorship of God. His address was very strong and had in it both argument and eloquence. He marshalled the Scriptures with consummate skill, and built an argument easily understood by the rudest of his hearers; and yet so compact and tactful was he, that his most cultured hearers bent beneath his force.

But the second question brought on the pyrotechnics. It had to do with the origin of sin,--"Whar sin kum frum?"--as he cogently put it. It was here that a riotous liberty possessed him and he preached with every faculty of his mind, with every passion and sentiment of his soul, with every nerve, every muscle, and every feature of his body. For nearly an hour the air cracked with excitement and the crowd melted beneath his spell. It was my first experience of that unusual power of his to move people in all possible ways by a single effort.

Jasper knew the fundamental doctrines of the Bible admirably, and always lived in vital contact with their essence. There was a kinship between the Bible and himself, and, untaught of the schools, he studied himself in the light of the Bible and studied the Bible in the darkness of himself. This kept him in contact with people and whenever he preached he invaded their experience and made conscious their wants to themselves. And so it came to pass that questions which perplexed them they had the habit of bringing to him. This question as to the origin of sin had been spurring and nagging some of his speculative hearers. They had wrangled over it, and they unloaded their perplexity upon him. So it was with this burden heavy upon him that he came to the pulpit on this occasion.

It may have been a touch of his dramatic art, but at any rate he showed an amiable irritation, in view of his being under constant fire from his controversial church-members, and so he started in as if he had a grievance. It gave pith and excitement to his bearing, as he faced the issue thus thrust upon him. As a fact, he knew that

many inquirers sought to entangle him by their questions and this opened the way for his saying, with cutting effect, that they would do better to inquire, "whar sin wuz gwine ter kerry 'em, instid uv whar it kum frum."

"An' yer wants ter know whar sin kum frum, yer say. Why shud yer be broozin' eroun' wid sich a questun as

dat? Dar ain' but wun place in de univus uv Gord whar
yer kin git any infermashun on dis pint, and dar, I am free
ter tel yer, yer kin git all dat yer wish ter know, an' maybe
a good deal mo'. De place whar de nollidge yer need kin
be got iz in de Word uv Gord. I knows wat sum dat hav'
bin talkin' 'bout dis thing iz arter. I know de side uv de
questun dey iz struttin' up on. Dey say, or dey kinder hint,
dat de Lord Gord iz de orthur uv sin. Dat's wat dey iz
wispurrin' roun' dis town. Dey can't fool Jasper; but I tell
you de debbul iz playin' pranks on um an' will drag um
down ter de pit uv hell, ef dey doan luk out mity quick.
De Lord Gord know'd frum de beginnin' dat sum uv dese
debbullish people wud bring up dis very charge an' say
dat He had tendid dat dar shud be sin frum de beginnin'.
He done speak His mind 'bout dat thing, an' ef yer luk in
de fust chaptur uv Jeems, yer'll find de solum uttrunce on
dis subjik an' it kleers Gord furevur frum dis base slandur.
'Let no man say,'says de Lord, 'wen he is temptid dat he is
temptid uv Gord, fur Gord kin not be temptid uv any man,
an' neethur tempts He any man.' Did yer hear dat? Dat's
de Lord's own wurds. It spressly says dat people will be
temptid, --everybody is temptid; I bin havin' my
temptashuns all my life, an' I haz um yit, a heap uv um,
an' sum uv um awful bad, but yer ain' ketchin' Jasper er
sayin' dat Gord is at de bottum uv um. Ef I shud say it, it
wud be a lie, an' all iz liars wen dey say dat Gord tempts
um? De sinnur is gettin' towurds de wust wen he iz willin'
ter lay de blame uv hiz sins on de Lord. Do it ef yer will,
but de cuss uv Gord will be erpun yez wen yer try ter mek

de Lord Gord sich es you iz; an' ter mek b'liev dat de Lord gits orf His throne an' kums down in ter mire an' clay uv your wicked life an' tries ter jog an' ter fool yer inter sin. I trimbul ter think uv sich a thing! I wonder dat de Lord duzn't forge new thunderbolts uv Hiz rath an' crush de heds uv dem dat charge 'im wid de folly uv human sin.

"Sum uv yer wud be mity glad ter git Gord mix'd up in yer sins an' ter feel dat He iz es bad es you iz. It jes' shows how base, how lost, how ded, you'se bekum. Wudn't we hev a pritty Gord ef He wuz willin' ter git out in de nite an' go plungin' down inter de horribul an' ruinus transgresshuns in wich sum men indulg'. Let me kleer dis thing up befo' I quit it. Bar in mine, dat Gord kin not be temptid uv any man.

Try it ef yer chuze, an' He will fling yer in ter de lowes' hell, an' don't yer dar evur ter say, or ter think, or ter hope, dat de temtashun ter du rong things kum ter yer from Gord. It do not kum frum erbuv, but it kum out uv your foul an' sinful hart. Dey iz born dar, born uv your bad thoughts, born uv your hell-born lusts, an' dey gits strong in yer 'caus' yer don't strangul um at de start.

"But why shud dar be trubble 'bout dis subjic? Wat duz de Bibul say on dis here mattur 'bout whar sin kum frum? We kin git de troof out uv dat buk, fur it kuntains de Wurd uv Gord. Our Gord kin not lie; He nevur hav' lied frum de foundashun uv de wurl'. He iz de troof an' de life an' He nevur lies.

"Now, wat do He say kunsarnin' dis serus questun dat is plowin' de souls uv sum uv my brudderin. Ter de Bibul, ter de Bibul, we'll go an' wat do we git wen we git dar? De Bibul say dat Eve wuz obur dar in de gardin uv Edun one day an' dat she wuz dar by hersef. De Lord med Eve, 'caus' it worn't gud fer Adum ter be erloan, an' it luks frum dis kase dat it wuz not quite safe fer Eve ter be lef' at home by hersef. But Adum worn't wid her; doan know whar he wuz,--gorn bogin' orf sumwhars. He better bin at home tendin' ter his fambly. Dat ain' de only time, by a long shot, dat dar haz bin de debbul ter pay at home wen de man hev gorn gaddin' eroun', instid uv stayin' at home an' lookin' arter hiz fambly.

"While Eve wuz sauntrin' an' roamin eroun' in de buterful gardin, de ole sarpint, dyked up ter kill, kum gallervantin' down de road an' he kotch'd site uv Eve an' luk lik he surpriz'd very much but not sorry in de leas'. Now yer mus' kno' dat ole sarpint wuz de trickies' an' de arties' uv all de beas' uv de feil',--de ole debbul, dat's wat he wuz. An' wat he do but go struttin' up ter Eve in a mity frien'ly way, scrapin' an' bowin' lik a fool ded in luv.

" 'How yer do?' He tries ter be perlite, an' puts on hiz sweetes' airs. Oh, dat wuz an orful momint in de life uv Eve an' in de histurry uv dis po' los' wurl uv ours. In dat momint de pizun eat thru her flesh, struk in her blud, an' went ter her hart. At fust she wuz kinder shame'; but she wuz kinder loansum, an' she wuz pleas'd an' tickl'd ter git notic'd in dat way an' so she stay'd dar instid uv runnin' fer her life.

" 'Ve'y wel, I thanks yer,' she say ertremblin', 'how iz you dis mornin'?' De sarpint farly shouts wid joy. He dun got her tenshun an' she lek ter hear 'im, an' he feel he got hiz chanz an' so goes on:

" 'Nice gardin yer got dar,' he say in er admirin' way. 'Yer got heap uv nice appuls obur dar.'

"'Oh, yes, indeed,'Eve replies. 'We got lots uv um.'

"Eve spoke dese wurds lik she wuz proud ter deth 'caus' de sarpint lik de gardin. Dar stood de sarpint ve'y quiut tel, suddin lek, he juk eroun' an' he says ter Eve: --

" 'Kin yer eat all de appuls yer got obur dar?'

"'No, hindeed,' says Eve, 'we can't eat um all. We got moar'n we kin 'stroy save our lives. Dey gittin' ripe all de time; we hev jus' hogshids uv um.'

"'Oh, I didn't mean dat,'spoke de sarpint, es ef shock'd by not bein' understud. 'My p'int iz, iz yer 'low'd ter eat um all? Dat's wat I want ter know. As ter yer laws an' rites in de gardin, duz dey all sute yer?'

"Fer a minnit de 'oman jump'd same es if sumbudy struk her a blow. De col' chils run down her bak, an' she luk lik she wan ter run, but sumhow de eye uv de sarpint dun got a charm on her. Dar wuz a struggul, er reglur Bull Run battul, gwine on in her soul at dat momint.

"'Wat yer ax me dat questun fur?' Eve axed, gaspin' w'ile she spoke. Den de debbul luk off. He tri ter be kam an' ter speak lo an' kine, but dar wuz a glar' in hiz eyes. 'I begs many parduns,' he says, 'skuse me, I did not mean ter meddul wid yer privit buzniz. I'd bettur skuse mysef, I reckin, and try an' git erlong.'

"'No; doan go,' Eve sed. 'Yer havn't hurt

my feelin's. Wat yer say jes' put new thoughts in my min' an' kinder shuk me up at fust. But I doan min' talkin'.'

"'Ef dat be de kase,' speaks up de debbul, quite brave-lek, 'begs you skuse me ter ask agin ef de rules uv de gardin 'lows yer ter eat any uv dem appuls yer got in de gardin? I haz my reasuns fer axin' dis.'

"Eve stud dar shivurrin' lik she freezin' an' pale es de marbul toomstoan. But arter a gud wile she pint her han obur to er tree, on de hill on de rite, an' she tel 'im, es ef she wuz mity 'fraid, dat dar wuz a tree obur dar uv de Nollidge an' uv de Deestinxshun, an' she say, 'De Lord Gord He tel us we mus' not eat dem appuls; dey pisun us, an' de day we eat um we got to die.'

"Oh, my brudderin, worn't times mity serus den? 'Twuz de hour wen de powurs uv darknis wuz gittin' in an' de foundashuns uv human hopes wuz givin' way. Den it wuz he git up close ter Eve an' wispur in her ear:--

" 'Did de Lord Gord tel yer dat? Doan tel nobody, but I wan' ter tel yer dat it ain't so. Doan yer b'liev it. Doan let 'im fool yer! He know dat's de bes' fruit in all de gardin,--de fruit uv de Nollidge an' de Deestinxshun, an' dat wen yer eats it yer will know es much es He do. Yer reckin He wants yer ter know es much es He do? Na-a-w; an' dat's why He say wat He do say. You go git um. Dey's de choysis' fruit in de gardin, an' wen yer eats um yer will be equ'ul ter Gord.'

"Erlas, erlas! po' deluded an' foolish Eve! It wuz de momint uv her evurlastin' downfall. Clouds uv darknis shrouds her min' an' de ebul sperrit leap inter her soul an' locks de do' behin' him. Dat dedly day she bruk 'way frum de Gord dat made her, Eve did, an' purtuk uv de fruit dat brought sin an' ruin an' hell inter de wurl'."

"Po' foolish Eve! In dat momunt darknis fils her min', evul leaps in ter er heart, an' she pluck de appul, bruk de kumman uv Gord, and ate de fatul fruit wat brought death ter all our race.

"Artur er wile, Adum kum walkin' up de gardin and Eve she runs out ter meet 'im. Wen he kum near she hol' up er appul in her han' and tell him it iz gud ter eat. Oh, blin' and silly womun! First deceived herself, she turn roun' and deceives Adum. Dat's de way; we gits wrong, an' den we pulls udder folks down wid us. We rarly goes down by oursefs.

"But whar wuz de rong? Whar, indeed? It wuz in Eve's believin' de debbul and not believin' Gord. It wuz doin' wat de debbul sed an' not doin' wat Gord sed. An' yer kum here and ax me whar sin kum frum! Yer see now, doan' sher? It kum out uv de pit uv hell whar it wuz hatched 'mong de ainjuls dat wuz flung out uv heav'n 'caus, dey disurbeyd Gord. It kum from dat land

whar de name uv our Gord is hated. It wuz brought by dat ole sarpint, de fathur uv lies, and he brung it dat he mite fool de woman, an' in dat way sot up on de urth de wurks uv de debbul. Sin iz de black chile uv de pit, it is. It kum frum de ole sarpint at fust, but it's here now, rite in po' Jasper's hart and in your hart; wharevur dar iz a man or a woman in dis dark wurl' in tears dar iz sin,--sin dat insults Gord, tars down His law, and brings woes ter evrybody.

"An' you, stung by de sarpint, wid Gord's rath on yer and yer feet in de paf uv deth, axin' whar sin kum frum? Yer bettur fly de rath uv de judgmint day.

"But dis iz ernuff. I jes' tuk time ter tell whar sin kum frum. But my tong carnt refuse ter stop ter tel yer dat de blud uv de Lam' slain frum de foundashun uv de wurl' is grettur dan sin and mitier dan hell. It kin wash erway our sins, mek us whitur dan de drivin snow, dress us in redemshun robes, bring us wid shouts and allerluejurs bak ter dat fellership wid our Fathur, dat kin nevur be brokin long ez 'ternity rolls."

This outbreak of fiery eloquence was not the event of the afternoon, but simply an incident. It came towards the end of the service, and its delivery took not much more time than is required to read this record of it. His language was perhaps never more broken; but what he said flamed with terrific light. While there were touches of humour in his description of the scene in the Garden, his message gathered a seriousness and solemnity which became simply overpowering. No words can describe the crushing and alarming effect which his weird story of the entrance of sin into the world had upon his audience. Men sobbed and fell to the floor in abject shame, and frightened cries for mercy rang wild through the church. Possibly never a sweeter gospel note sounded than that closing reference which he made to the cleansing power of the blood shed from the foundation of the world.

There were many white persons present, and they went away filled with a sense of the greatness and power of the Gospel.

VI
JASPER SET FREE

JASPER came to the verge of his greatness after he had passed the half century line. Freedom had come and to him brought nothing except the opportunity to carve out his own fortune. His ministry had been migratory, restricted and chiefly of un-gathered fruit. He found himself in Richmond without money and without a home. By daily toil he was picking up his bread. He was dead set on doing something in the way he wanted to do it. He was of the constructive sort, and never had done well when building on another man's foundation.

His ambition was to build a church. Down on the James River, where the big furnaces were run, there was a little island, and on the island a little house, and scattered along the canal and river were many of the newly liberated and uncared for people of his race.

He began to hold religious services on the island,-- said by some to have been held in a private house, and by others in a deserted stable, which was fitted up to accommodate the increasing crowds. Things went well with him. The joy of building flamed his soul, and beneath the tide of the river he baptized many converts. Happy days they were! The people were wild with enthusiasm, and the shouts of his congregation mingled with the noise of the James River Falls. It was to Jasper as the gate of heaven, and he walked as the King's ambassador among his admiring flock.

But it could not be that way long. There was not room enough to contain the people, and yet the church was poverty itself, and what could they do? Happily they found a deserted building beyond the canal and accessible to the growing company of his lovers in the city. There things went with a snap and a roar. From every quarter the people came to hear this African Boanerges. The crowds and songs and riotous shouts of his young church filled the neighborhood. Constant processions, with Jasper at the head, visited the river or canal, to give baptism to the multiplying converts.

Meanwhile, however, the northern part of the city was fast becoming the Africa of Richmond. Into its meaner outskirts at first the tide began to roll, but in a little while the white people began to retreat, street after street, until a vast area was given up to the coloured people. Jasper's people, also, as they prospered, began to settle in this new Africa, and Jasper found once more that he was simply dwelling in tents, when the time was coming for the building of the temple.

Jasper was on the outlook for a new location. Finally he hit upon an old brick church building, at the corner of Duval and St. John Streets. The Presbyterians, who had started this mission years before, had despaired of success under the changed conditions and they offered the house for sale, the price being $2,025. The sense of growth and progress fairly maddened this unique and fascinating preacher with enthusiasm. He had found a home for his people at last, and yet, in point of fact, he had not. The house was a magnificent gain on their old quarters, and yet Sunday afternoon found most of his crowd every on the outside. Quite soon his people had to enlarge and remodel the house, and this they did at a cost of $6,000. By that time the membership was well on towards 2,000. There they dwelt for a number of years until the church became the center of the religious life in that part of the town. "John Jasper," as he was universally called, had easily become the most attractive and popular minister of his race in the city. By this time he was over sixty years of age, and it would have taken much to have quenched the yet un-wasted buoyancy and vitality of his ministry. Necessity demanded another building, and in the later prime of his kingly manhood, and very largely by his personal forcefulness and intrepid leadership, he led a movement for a house of worship that would be respectable in almost any part of Richmond. What was more to his purpose, it was very capacious, wisely adapted to the wants of his people and a fitting monument to his constructive resource and enthusiasm. It is said that he, out of his own slender resources, gave $3,000 to the building fund, and this was probably in addition to great sums of money given him by white people who went to hear him preach and who delighted to honour and cheer the old man. I suppose that thousands of dollars were given him from no motive save that of kindness towards him, and the donours would just as soon have given the money directly to him and for his own use. They helped to build the church simply to please the old man whose eloquence and honesty had won their hearts. His love for his church amounted to devotion. He had seen it grow from the most insignificant beginning, had watched the tottering steps of its childhood, and with pride natural and affectionate had gloried in its prosperity.

But be it said to the old man's honour that he was too great to be conceited. He had no sense of boastfulness or self-glorification about the church. He had the frankness to tell the truth about things when it was necessary, but he had too much manly modesty to claim distinction for the part he had borne in the building up of the church. Indeed, he was strangely silent about his relations with the church, and his dominant feeling was one of affectionate solicitude for the future of the church rather than of self-satisfaction on account of its history.

There was a strain of severity in Jasper. He had some of the temper of the reformer. He was quick,--often too quick--in condemning those who criticised him. The fact is, he was so unfeignedly honest that he could not be patient towards those whose sincerity or honesty he doubted. For those who plotted against the church or gave trouble in other ways he had little charity. Those that would not work in harness, and help to move things along, he was quite willing to show to the church door.

For his part, he could not love those very warmly who did not love the "Sixth Mount Zion."

This may be the right place to say a word or two as to Jasper's enemies. He was a man of war, and it may be that his prejudices sometimes got in the saddle. But not very often. Possibly, his most striking characteristic was his bottom sense of justice. He told the truth by instinct, and it never occurred to him to take an undue advantage. If, however, a man wronged him, he was simply terrible in bringing the fellow to book. There was a case, in which it is better not to mention names, in which an insidious and grievous accusation was brought against this sturdy old friend of the faith. The charge sought to fasten falsehood upon Jasper. That was enough for him,--it amounted to a declaration of war, and at once he entered upon the conflict. Never did he cease the strife until the charge was unsaid. Nothing, in short, could terrify him.

It must not be inferred that those who assailed him with questions and arguments were put into the category of personal enemies. Controversy was exactly to his taste. All he asked of the other man was to state his proposition, and he was ready for the contest. Not that he went into it pell-mell. By no means; he took time for preparation, and when he spoke it was hard to answer him. This, of course, applies when the questions were theological and Scriptural, and not scientific. His knowledge of the Scriptures was remarkable, and his spiritual insight into the doctrines of the Bible was extraordinary. When he preached, he supported every point with Scriptural quotations, invariably giving the chapter and verse, and often adding, "Ef yer don' find it jes' ezackly ez I tells yer, yer kin meet me on de street nex' week an' say ter me: 'John Jasper, you ar er lier,' an' I won' say er wurd."

What gave to Jasper an exalted and impressive presence was his insistent claim that he was a God-sent man. This he asserted in almost every sermon, and with such evident conviction that he forced other people to believe it. Even

those who differed with him were constrained to own his sincerity and Godliness. It was impossible to be with him much without being impressed that he was anointed of God for his work. It was in this that his people gloried. Their faith in him was preeminent,--far above every question--and he was also full of inspiration. You may talk with his disciples now, wherever you meet them, and they are quick to tell you that "Brer Jasper was certainly aninted uv God," and even the more intelligent of the people ascribed his greatness to the fact that he was under the power of the Holy Ghost. Many wicked people heard him preach, and some of them still went their wicked way, but they felt that the power of God was with Jasper, and they were always ready to say so. In many points, John Jasper was strikingly like John the Baptist,--a just man and holy, and the people revered him in a way I never met with in any other man.

VII
THE PICTURE-MAKER

IN the circle of Jasper's gifts his imagination was preeminent. It was the mammoth lamp in the tower of his being. A matchless painter was he. He could flash out a scene, colouring every feature, defining every incident and unveiling every detail. Time played no part in the performance,--it was done before you knew it. Language itself was of second moment. His vocabulary was poverty itself, his grammar a riot of errors, his pronunciation a dialectic wreck, his gestures wild and unmeaning, his grunts and heavings terrible to hear. At times he hardly talked but simply emitted; his pictures were simply himself in flame. His entire frame seemed to glow with living light, and almost wordlessly he wrought his miracles. But do not misunderstand. Some insisted on saying that education would have stripped John of his genius by subduing the riot of his power and chastening the fierceness of his imagination. I think not, for John in a good sense was educated. He was a reverential and laborious student for half-a-century. He worked on his sermons with a marked assiduity and acquired the skill and mastership of faithful struggle. Even his imagination had to work, and its products were the fruit of toil. There was no mark of the abnormal or disproportionate in his sky, but all the stars were big and bright. He was well ballasted in his mental make-up, and in his most radiant pictures there was an ethical regard for facts, and an instinctive respect for the truth. Moreover, his ministrations fairly covered the theological field, were strongly doctrinal, and he grappled with honest vigor the deepest principles of the Gospel. He was also intensely practical, scourging sin, lashing neglect, and with lofty authority demanding high and faithful living.

Think not of Jasper merely as a pictorial preacher. There were wrought into his pictures great principles and rich lessons. But now and then he would present a sermon which was largely a series of pictures from beginning to end. His imagination would be on duty all the time and yet never flag. I cannot forget his sermon on Joseph and his Brethren. It was a stirring presentation of the varied scenes in that memorable piece of history. He opened on the favoritism of Jacob, and was exceedingly strong in condemning partiality, as unhappily expressed in the coat of many colours. That brief part was a sermon itself for parents. From that he passed quickly to the envy of his brothers. jealousy was a demon creeping in among them, inflicting poisonous stings, and spreading his malignant power, until murder rankled in every heart. Then came Joseph, innocent and ignorant of offending, to fall a victim to their conspiracy, with the casting of him into the pit, the selling of him to the travelling tradesmen, the showing to Jacob of the blood-stained coat, with scene after scene until the happy meeting at last between Jacob and his long lost son.

One almost lived a lifetime under the spell of that sermon. It was eloquent, pathetic, terrific in its denunciations, rich in homely piety, and with strains of sweetness that was as balm to sorrowing souls. The effects were as varied as human thoughts and sentiments. The audience went through all moods. Now they were bent down as if crushed with burdens; now they were laughing in tumults at the surprises and charms of heavenly truth; anon they were sobbing as if all hearts were broken, and in a moment hundreds were on their feet shaking hands, shouting, and giving forth snatches of jubilant song. This all seems extravagant, without sobriety entirely, but those that were there, perhaps without an exception, felt that it was the veritable house of God and the gate of heaven.

At other times, Jasper's sermons were sober and deliberate, sometimes even dull; but rarely did the end come without a burst of eloquence or an attractive, entertaining picture. But, remember, that his pictures were never foreign to his theme. They were not lugged in to fill up. They had in them the might of destiny and fitted their places, and fitted them well. Often they came unheralded, but they were evidently born for their part. On one occasion his sermon was on Enoch. It started out at a plodding gait and seemed for a time doomed to dullness, for Jasper could be dull sometimes. At one time he brought a smile to the faces of the audience, in speaking of Enoch's age, by the remark: "Dem ole folks back dar cud beat de presunt ginerashun livin' all ter pieces."

As he approached the end of his sermon, his face lighted up and took on a new grace and passion, and he went out with Enoch on his last walk. That walk bore him away to the border of things visible; earthly scenes were lost to view; light from the higher hills gilded the plains. Enoch caught sight of the face of God, heard the music and the shouting of a great host, and saw the Lamb of God seated on the throne. The scene was too fair to lose, and Enoch's walk quickened into a run which landed him in his father's house. It was a quick, short story, told in soft and mellow tones, and lifted the audience up so far that the people shouted and sang as if they were themselves entering the gates of heaven.

One of his more elaborate descriptions, far too rich to be reproduced, celebrated the ascension of Elijah. There was the oppressive unworldliness of the old prophet, his efforts to shake off Elisha, and Elisha's wise persistence in clamouring for a blessing from his spiritual father. But it was when the old prophet began to ascend that Jasper, standing off like one apart from the scene, described it so thrillingly that everything was as plain as open day. To the people, the prophet was actually and visibly going away. They saw him quit the earth, saw him rise above the mountain tops, sweeping grandly over the vast fields of space, and finally saw him as he passed the moon and stars. Then something happened. In the fraction of a second Jasper was transmuted into Elijah and was actually in the chariot and singing with extraordinary power the old chorus: "Going up to heaven in a chariot of fire." The scene was overmastering! For a time I thought that Jasper was the real Elijah, and my distinct feeling was that the song which he sang could be heard around the world. Of course, it was not so; but there was something in the experience of the moment that has abided with me ever since.

At a funeral one Sunday I saw Jasper attempt a dialogue with death, himself speaking for both. The line of thought brought him face to face with death and the grave. The scene was solemnized by a dead body in a coffin. He put his hands over his mouth and stooped down and addressed death. Oh, death--death, speak to me. Where is thy sting? And then with the effect of a clairvoyant he made reply: "Once my sting was keen and bitter, but now it is gone. Christ Jesus has plucked it out, and I have no more power to hurt His children. I am only the gatekeeper to open the gateway to let His children pass." In closing this chapter an incident will largely justify my seemingly extraordinary statements as to the platform power of this unschooled negro preacher in Virginia.

In company with a friend I went very often Sunday afternoons to hear Jasper and the fact was bruited about quite extensively, and somewhat to the chagrin of some of my church-members. Two of them, a professor in Richmond College and a lawyer well-known in the city, took me to task about it They told me in somewhat decided tones that my action was advertising a man to his injury, and other things of a similar sort. I cared but little for their criticism, but told them that if they would go to hear him when he was at his best, and if afterwards they felt about him as they then felt, I would consider their complaints. They went the next Sunday. The house was overflowing, and Jasper walked the mountain tops that day. His theme was "The raising of Lazarus" and by steps majestic he took us along until he began to describe the act of raising Lazarus from the dead. It happened that the good professor was accompanied by his son, a sprightly lad of about ten, who was sitting between his father and myself. Suddenly the boy, evidently agitated, turned to me and begged that we go home at once. I sought to soothe him, but all in vain, for as he proceeded the boy urgently renewed his request to go home. His father observed his disquietude and putting an arm around him restored him to calmness. After the service ended and we had reached the street, I said to him: "Look here, boy, what put you into such a fidget to quit the church before the end of the service?" "Oh, doctor, I thought he had a dead man under the pulpit and was going to take him out," he said. My lawyer brother heard the sermon and with profound feeling said, "Hear that, and let me say to you that in a lifetime I have heard nothing like it, and you ought to hear that man whenever you can."

I heard no later criticisms from any man concerning my conduct in evincing such cordial interest in this eloquent son of Fluvanna.

It was only necessary to persuade Jasper's critics to hear him, to remove all question as to his genuine character and effective spiritual ministry.

VIII
JASPER'S STAR WITNESS

THE domestic history of this rare and gifted man was not without its tragical incidents. One of the worst features of slavery, as an institution in the South, was the inevitable legislation which it necessitated, and under which many grievous wrongs were perpetrated. The right of the slave owner to the person of the slave carried with it the authority to separate man and wife at the dictate of self-interest, and that was often done, though it ought to be said that thousands of kindhearted men and women did their utmost to mitigate the wrongs which such legislation legalized. In the sale of the negroes regard was often had for the marriage relation, and it was arranged so that the man and wife might not be tom asunder. But it was not always this way. Too often the sanctity of marriage and the laws of God concerning it were sacrificed to the greed of the slaveholder.

If the tradition of Mr. Jasper's first marriage is to be accepted as history, then he was the victim of the cruel laws under which the institution of slavery was governed. In the changes which came to him in the breaking up of the family to which he belonged his lot was cast for a while in the city of Williamsburg. The story is that he became enamoured of a maiden bearing the name of Elvy Weaden, and he was successful in his suit. It chanced, however, that on the very day set for his marriage, he was required to go to Richmond to live. The marriage was duly solemnized and he was compelled to leave his bride abruptly, but was buoyed with the hope that fairer days would come when their lot would be cast together. The fleeting days quenched the hope and chilled the ardour of the bride, and in course of time the impatient woman notified Jasper that unless he would come to see her and they could live together, she would account herself free to seek another husband. He was not a man to brook mistreatment, and he made short work of the matter. He wrote her that he saw no hope of returning to Williamsburg, and that she must go ahead and work out her own fate. Naturally enough, the difficulties under which the married life had to be maintained served to weaken seriously the marital tie and to imperil the virtue of the slaves. But this remark ought not to be made without recalling the fact that there were thousands and tens of thousands of happy and well-governed families among the slaves of the South.

Jasper felt seriously the blight of this untimely marriage and he seems to have remained unmarried until after he united with the church and became a preacher. In time, his thoughts turned again to marriage. He was then a member of the First African Baptist Church of Richmond. He took the letter which his wife had written him some time before and presented it to the church and asked what was his duty under the circumstances. It was a complex and vexing question, but his brethren, after soberly weighing the matter, passed a resolution expressing the conviction that it would be entirely proper for him to marry again. Accordingly, about five years after his conversion, he married a woman bearing the unusual name of Candus Jordan. According to all reports, this marriage was far more fruitful in children than in the matter of connubial peace and bliss for the high-strung and ambitious Jasper. It seems that the case must have had some revolting features, as in due time Jasper secured a divorce and was fully justified by his brethren and friends in taking this action. Evidently this separation from his wife, which was purely voluntary, in no way weakened him in the confidence and good-will of the people.

Years after his divorce, Jasper married Mrs. Mary Anne Cole. There were no children by this marriage, but his wife had a daughter by her former marriage who took the name of Jasper, and was adopted in fact and in heart as the daughter of this now eminent and beloved minister. This wife died in 1874, and Jasper married once more. His widow survived him and still lives, a worthy and honoured woman whose highest earthly joy is the recollection of having been the wife of Elder John Jasper, and also the solace and cheer of his old age. This is a checkered story of a matrimonial career, but justice loudly demands the statement that through it all John Jasper walked the lofty path of virtue and honour. It was impossible, however, for a man like Jasper to escape the arrows of the archer. Jealousy, envy, and slander were often busy with his name, and if foul charges could have befouled him none could have been fouler than he. But his daily life was a clean and unanswerable story. Reproaches would not stick to him, and the deadliest darts fell harmless at his feet. His noble seriousness, his absorption in the study of the Bible, his enthusiasm in the ministry, and, most of all, his quiet walk with God, saved him from the grosser temptations of life.

Perhaps the finest incident in all the story of his life was the perfect faith of the people in Jasper. This was true everywhere that he was known, but it was most powerfully true among those who stood nearest to him and knew him best. Jasper, to them, was the incarnation of goodness. They felt his goodness, revelled in it, and lived on it. Their best earthly inspirations sprang out of the fair and incorruptible character of their pastor. If his enemies sought to under mine and defame him, they rallied around him and fought his battles. Little cared he for the ill things said about him personally. Conscious of his rectitude, and, embosomed in the love of his great church, he walked serenely and triumphantly in the way of the Lord. He believed in the sanctity of his home, and he hallowed it by the purity, honesty, and charity of his brethren.

Anxious to get some living testimony in regard to the personal character of Jasper, I determined to get in contact with a few persons who stood very close to him, and that, for many years. In what follows is found the testimony of a truly excellent woman, to whom I was directed, with the assurance that what she said might be taken as thoroughly trustworthy. She gave her name as Virginia Adams, and, judging from her appearance and manner, one would probably write her down as not far from threescore and ten. She was for many years a member of his church. The following story from her lips is not connected, but it is simply the unmethodical testimony of a sensible woman, bearing about it the marks of sincerity, intelligence, and reverential affection.

"Brer' Jasper was as straightfor'd a man es you cud see, and yer cud rely 'pon ev'ry word he told yer. He made it so plain dat watuver he tol' yer in his sermon yer cud read it right thar in yer heart, jes' like he had planted and stamped it in yer. I can't read myse'f, but I kno' well when anybody mek any mistake 'bout de passages which Brer Jasper used to preach 'bout. I've got 'em jes' de same es if I had 'em printed on my mem'ry. His mi'ty sermon on Elijer is in me jes' es he preached it. I kin see Elijer es Elisha is runnin' arter him,--kin see de cheryot es it kum down, see Brer Jasper es he wuz pintin' ter de cheryot es it riz in its grand flight up de skies,--see Elijer es he flung his mantul out es he went up, and I tell yer when Brer Jasper began ter sing 'bout goin' up ter heaven in a cheryot uv fire I cud see everything jes' es bright es day, and de people riz such a shout dat I thought all de wurl' wuz shoutin'. Yes, Brer Jasper wuz de kindes' man I reckon on de urth. Yer cudn't finish tellin' him 'bout folks dat wuz in trouble and want, befo' he'd be gittin' out his money. He didn't look lik he keer much 'bout money,--he warn't no money-seeker, and yit he look lik he allus hev money, and he wuz allus de fust ter give. Jes' tell him wat wuz needed, and he begun fer to scratch in his pocket.

"Brer Jasper kep' things lively. People wuz talkin' all de time 'bout his sermons, and yer cud hear their argiments while yer wuz gwine 'long de streets. Often his members an' udder folks too wud git tangled up 'bout his doctrines and dey wud git up texs an' subjiks an' git him ter preach 'bout 'em. Ef any uv his brutherin had trubbul wid passiges uv de scripshur and went ter him 'bout 'em, you'd sure hear frum him nex Sunday. He luv ter splain things fer his brutherin.

"It wuz Bruther Woodson, de sexton uv de church, and anudder man dat got Brer Jasper in ter dat gret 'citemint 'bout de sun. Dey got inter a spute es to wheddur de sun went 'roun' de wurl' ur not, and dey took it ter our pastor, and really I thought I nevur wud hear de end of dat thing. Folks got arter Brer Jasper in de papurs, and everywhar; but I tell yer dey nevur skeered him. He wuz es brave es a lion, an' I don' kno' how often he preached dat sermon. It look lik all de people in de wurl' want to kum.

"No, Brer Jasper wuz no money-grabbur. When de church wuz weak and cudn't raze much money, he nevur sot no salary. Yer cudn't git him ter do it. He tell 'em not ter trubble 'emselves, but jes' giv him wat dey chuze ter put in de baskit and he nevur made no kumplaint. Wen de church got richer dey crowd 'im hard ter kno' how much he wantid, and he at las' tell 'em dat he wud take $62.50 a month, and dat he didn't want no more dan dat. Wen de gret crowds got ter kummin' and de white folks too, and de money po'ed in so fas' de brutherin farly quarl'd wid him ter git his sal'ry raz'd, but he say No I git nuff now, and I want no more. I'm not here to gouge my people out of es much money es I kin. He say he got nuff money to pay his taxes and buy wat he needed, and if dey got more dan dey wantid let 'em take it and help de Lord's pore. Sometimes we used ter 'poun'' de ole man, kerryin' 'im all kinds uv good things ter eat. He didn't lik it at all, but tuk de things and sont 'em 'roun' ter de pore people.

"Brer Jasper wuz nun uv yer parshul preachers. His church wuz his family, and he had no favrites. He did not bow down ter de high nor hol' 'imsef 'bove de low. Enny uv his people cud kum ter him 'bout all dere struggles and sorrers. He hated erroneyus doctrines. His faith in de Bibul wuz powerful, and he luved it 'bove everything. He had awful dreds 'bout wat mite kum ter de church wen he wuz gone. He sometimes said in a mity solem way, 'Wen I am daid and gone, yer will look out ter whar my ashes lay and wish I wuz back here ter 'part ter yer de pure wurd uv Gord agin. I got a fear dat dose dat kum arter me will try ter pull down wat I built up. I pray Gord, my children will stand by de ship uv Zion wen I's gone.'

"Brer Jasper got troubles 'bout de way young childun wuz got inter de church. He say 'all yer got ter do is to pitty-pat em (making the motion in the pulpit with his hands) on dere haids and dey are in de kingdom. Sum uv yer duz the convertin' of dese little uns instid er leavin' it ter God ter do de work.' He believed in regenerashum of folks. He preach'd ter de very last on being born agin, and he didn't want nobody ter kum inter his church wat ain't felt de power uv de sperrit in dere souls.

"But Brer Jasper wuz a mity luver uv de childun. He had a great way of stoppin' and talkin' ter dem on de street. He wuz a beaudful story-teller, and de childrun often flocked ter his house ter hear 'im tell nice stories and all kine uv good tales. He kept pennies in his pockets and often dropped 'em along for de chilrun--he had great ways,--til de chilrun ud think he wuz de greatest man dat ever put foot on de yearth.

"Brer Jasper wuz sosherbul wid everybody, and nobody cud beat him as a talker. He knew lots 'bout Richmond, and de ole times, and he had de grandest stories and jokes dat he luved ter tell and dat de folks went wild ter hear. He wuz great on jokes and cracked 'em in sech a funny way dat folks most killed de 'sefs laughin'. But yer mus' kno' dat he wuz mity keerful 'bout how he talked. Yer neer hear no bad words frum his mouth. His stories he could tell ennywhar, and wuz jes' as nice ter de ladies as ter der men. He didn't b'leve in no Sercities. Dey tried ter git 'im in de Masons, and I don't kno' wat all, but he ain't tech none uv 'em. He sez dar ain't but one Grand Past Master and dat is King Jesus.

"Dey orf'n wanted 'im at de big public suppers war
dey et an' drank an' made speeches, but he wouldn't go
near; and den our high people had der big suppers in dere
houses and wanted de 'onur uv enteitainin' Brer Jasper,
but he didn't hanker arter dose kind uv things. He wanted
his meals simple and reglur and uv de plain sort, and as
fer dese high ferlootin' feasts dey didn't suit his taste.

"It look lik Brer Jasper couldn't stop preachin'. It
wuz his food and drink, an' enny time he'd git way
beyond his strength. I've seen 'im wen it looked lik de las'
bref hed gone out'en his body, and sometimes some uv de
brutherin say he did not look like a natchul man. He
seemed more in hevun dan on urth. I most reckun some
uv de brutherin thought he wuz gone up in ter heavun like
Lijer. Dey go in de pulpit and tek hol' uv 'im and say Brer
Jasper yer dun preached nuff. Don't wear yerself down.
Tek yer seat and res' yersef. He knew dey did it fer luv,
and he took it kind, but he didn't always stop at once.

"Brer Jasper had a walk mity remarkbul. Wen he
went in de streets he wuz so stately and grave lik dat he
walk diffrunt from all de people. Folks wud run out uv all
de stores, or out on der porches, or turn back ter look wen
Jasper kum, 'long. Oh, it made us proud ter look at him.
No other preacher could walk like him. Yer felt de ground
got holy war he went 'long. Sum uv 'em say it wuz ekul
ter a revival ter see John Jasper moving lik a king 'long de
street. Often he seemed ter be wrappd up in his thoughts
and hardly to know whar he wuz. De people feared 'im so

much,--wid sech a luvin' kind uv fear, dat dey hardly dared to speak ter him.

"Brer Jasper wuz mity fond uv walkin' in de pulpit. It wuz a great large place, and he frisked round most lik he wuz a boy. Wen he filled up wid de rousement of the Gospel on him, it was just glor'us to see him as he whirled about the stand; the faces of his folks shone wid de brightness of de sun, and they ofen made the house ring with laughter and with their shouts.

"One thing he did dat always made his congregasons rock wid joy, an' dat wuz ter sing wile he wuz preachin'. He wuz mos' ninety years old, but he never lost his power ter sing, an' wen he struck er tune de note uv it shot in de people lik arrurs from anguls quivur. Yer cudn't hol' still wen Jasper sung. Soon as he started, de people would 'gin to swing an' jine in tel de music filled de house. He cud sing a heap uv songs, but he had a few great songs. Yer orter to hear him sing by hiself his favrite piece." Here it is:

EV'BUDY GOT TER RISE TER MEET KING JESUS IN DE MORNIN'

"'Ev'budy got ter rise ter meet King Jesus in de mornin';
De high and de lo';
De rich and de po',

De bond and de free,
As well as me.

"'Yer got ter rise ter meet King Jesus in de mornin',
Weddur yer iz purparred er no,
Ter Gord's trirbewnul
Yer got ter go,
Yer got ter rise ter meet King Jesus in de mornin'.

"'De lurnid and de unlurnid,
Barbareun, Jentile and de Jew,
Hev yer red hit in Hiz wurd,
Dat de peepul wuz drondid in de flud,
Ev'budy got ter rise ter meet King Jesus in de mornin'.'

"Dar wuz a song dat Jasper made hisself. Some
called it a ballard, and udders said it wuz a poem; but wat
evur twuz, it wuz glory ter hear him sing it. It went dis
way:--

"'I beheld and lo
A grate multertude dat no man kin number,
Thousuns and thousuns, an' ten thousun times ten
thousun,
Standin' befo' de Lam',
And dey had pams in dere hans.

"'Dey nevur restid day nur night,
Cryin' Holy, Holy, Holy, iz de Lord, Gord uv
Sabbuth
Dat wuz, an' iz, and iz ter kum,

 I saw a mi'ty ainjel flyin' through de midst uv
heaven,
Cryin' wid a loud voice,
Sayin' Woe! Woe! Woe! be unto de earth by reazun
uv de trumpit,
Dat which is yet ter soun'.
And when de las' trumpit shall soun',
See de great men and noble,
De rich, and de po', de bond and de free,
Gueddur 'emselves terguedder, cryin' ter de rocks,
an' ter de mountins,
Ter fall 'pon 'em an' hide 'em,
From de face uv Him dat sitteth on de throne,
De great day uv His rath hav kum an' who shall be
able ter stan'?'

"And den, too, he had his shoutin' song. He never
sung it 'cept wen de heavenly fires wuz burnin' all over
his soul. He kept tune wid his walkin' and wid de clappin'
uv his hands. Dis song never got in 'cept at de close uv
sermons dat had heaven in 'em, and somehow he jumped
from de sermon all at once in ter de song an' it would hev
fairly kilt yer wid joy ter hear it. Here is de way he put it:-
-

"'My soul will mount higher in a chariot of fire,
And de wurl' is put under my feet.'

Dis wuz the start uv it, but dere wuz heaps more.

"It wuz an awful time ter us wen we begun ter see
dat our ole pastor wuz near ter de end uv his race. We had
been a-dreddin' it by degrees and it broke on us more and
more. I think de dere man tried ter git us reddy fer it. He
kep sayin' to us: 'My chilrun, my work on de earth is dun.
I doan ask death no more odds dan a horse-fly.' But den
he'd preach so powerful dat we'd hope dat he'd hol' out a
good deal longer. He said ter me one day: 'Compartivly
speakin', my time in dis wurl' is skin deep,' and I look at
my hand and think how thin de skin is, and I feel dat sho'
nuff he mus' soon be goin'.

"One night at de church he turned hissef loos. He
said dat as fer 'imself it mattered nuthin'. He had paid all
his debts, dat he did not keer whar or when he dropped;
but he wanted everybody ter know dat he wud be wid
Jesus. Dat wuz one uv de things dat he luved ter say. Den
he told de church dat dar wuz nuthin' lef' uv him,--dat he
wanted 'em to git tergedder and pay off der church debt
and live tergedder lik little chil'run He wuz mity gret dat
night, an' it looked lik de powers uv de wurl' ter kum wuz
dar.

"De people went out silent lik an' dey said dat de gud
ole pastor preached his own funeral dat night. He allus

thought uv hissef es de servant uv King Jesus. Dat wuz a slavery dat he liked and nevur wished to git free from it. Towards de las' he wuz all de time sayin': 'I am now at de river's brink and waitin' fer furder orders. It's de same ter me ter go or stay, jes' es Gord commands '

"Some folks said dat he wuz conceited. Dey did not know him. He wuz too full uv de fear uv Gord to think he wuz sum great body, an' he know'd his own sins an' troubles too well ter boast. He must hev known dat Gord made him more uv a man dan de gen'ral run. He had ter kno' dat, 'caus' it wuz proved ter him every day, an' in a heap uv ways. Besides dat, he hilt hisself up high. He had good respec' for hisself and felt dat a man lik he wuz had got ter behave hisself 'cordin' ter wat he wuz. But dat wuz very different from bein' one uv dese giddy little fops dat is always trancin' aroun' showin' hisself off, and braggin' 'bout everything. I often wondered how Jasper could be so umble lik, wen so many cacklin' fools wuz bodderin' 'im.

"Brer Jasper could git up big things wen he tried. Wen dey got in a tight place 'bout de church an' had to have money, he got up a skurshun ter Washington. He sent out de members ter sell tickets, an' dey sold so many dat dey had ter have two trains ter carry 'em, and jes' think, sir, he cleared $1,500 fer his church by dat skurshun, and he got up anudder to Staunton dat wuz mos' as good as de udder one. Ah, he wuz a leader, I tell you he wuz. We never could have had our fine church if it had not bin fer him.

"It's mity easy fer folks ter forget things. Some folks are teerin' 'roun' as if the church b'longed ter 'em now, and dey are ready ter tell you dat Jasper made mistakes and all dat, but sum uv us knows well dat Jasper built dat church. You need nevur spect ter hear any more sech preachin' in dat pulpit as dat grand ole man uv God used ter give us.

"You know Brer Jasper got convicted uv his sins fer de first time on de 4th of July in Capitol Squar', Richmond. He use ter tell us 'bout it many a time. While de folks wuz swarmin' 'roun' and laffin' and hurrahin', an arrer uv convicshun went in ter his proud heart an' brought 'im low. He never forgot dat place, and when he got ter be an ole man he wuz kinder drawn ter Capitol Squar. He luv ter go down dar. He like de cool shade uv de trees and 'joyed de res', dozin' sometimes wen he wuz tired. De people, and speshully de chilrun, used ter git 'roun' him an' ask him questions an' make him talk. He lik things lik dat. Some uv de Jews used ter kum ter hear Brer Jasper preach. They called him Father Abraham and showed gret gud feelin' fur 'im. Some uv 'em used ter meet him in de Cap'tol Squar' an' dey would have great ole talks tergudder, an' he didn't mind tellin' 'em de truth an' he told 'em dat dey wuz de chilrun uv Abraham, but dat dey had gone all to pieces.

"Dey tell me he never went ter skule 'cep' six months, an' I hear dat he jes' studied wid a man dat taught him in a New York Speller book; but when he spoke at de Y. M. C. A. and many uv de white gemmen went ter hear 'im, they say he certainly used ellergunt language. I know he could handle great words when he wanted to, an' he could talk in de old way, an' he often loved to do dat."

IX
JASPER'S SERMON ON "DEM SEBUN WIMMIN"

"DID yer ebur git yer mine on wat Iz'er say in chapter fo' an' vurs wun? Listen ter hiz wurds: 'An' sebun wimmin shall tek hol' uv wun man in dat day, sayin' we will eat our own bread an' wear our own 'parrel; only let us be called by Thy name; tek Thou erway our reproach.' De Profit iz furloserfizin' 'bout de mattur uv wimmin,-- speshully wen dar is sebun in de lan', wen wars dun thin out de men and de wimmins feels de stings an' bites uv reproach. I tell yer, yer bettur not fling yer gibes an' sneers at er 'omun. She wuzn't made ter stan' it, an' wats mo', she ain't gwine ter stan' it. Shure ez yer iz settin' on dat bench she will fly erway an' hide hersef, or she will fly at yer, an' den, ole fellur, yer had bettur be pullin' out fer de tall timbur fast. Gord dun settled it dat wun 'omun iz nuff fer a man, an' two iz er war on yer hans,--bles yer, it is.

"But dar kums times wen it goze hard wid wimmin. Dey iz lef out uv de lottry uv heavun,--dey draws blanks an' dey gits ter be a laughin' stock uv de ungodly. Not dat dey iz crazy ter marry an' not dat dey iz uv dat flautin', slatturn lot dat's allus gallantin' eroun' ertryin' ter git a man ter 'sport um. Dese wuz squar, alrite wimmin. Wurk wud not skeer um. Dey wuz willin' ter mek dere bread an' cloes, ter pay dere own way, purvidid dey cud be Mrs.

Sumbody, an' in dat way 'skape de dev'lish jeers an' slites uv base men. Fur my part, I feels quite sorry fur dat class uv ladiz, an' I kinder feels my blud grittin' up wen I finds folks castin' reproachiz on dere fair names.

"But my mastur in de skies! Dis pikshur here uv de Profit iz too much fer me. It mek me feel lik tekin' ter de woods, in quick ordur. Lord, wat wud I do ef I wuz pursued by er army uv seben wimmin axin me ter 'low each wun uv um ter be call'd Mrs. Jasper? It may be dat each wun wuz fer hersef ter de limit, an' hoped ter shet out de udder six an' hev de man ter hersef;--an' ef she wuz ter hev 'im ertall she ort ter hav all uv im. Dar iz not nuff ter d'vide; I tel yer, dar ain't, an' wen yer git er haf intrest in er man yer iz po' indeed, an' ef only wun sevunth iz yourn, yer had es wel start on ter de po'house 'fo yer git yer dinner.

"A gud 'omun can't byar ter be oberluked. It ain't her nature, an' it iz a site fer de anguls ter see wat sort uv men sum wimmin wil tek sooner dan be lef out inti'ly.

"But wat gits me arter all iz a man. I see 'im in de quiet uv de day,--de Sabbuth day. He

teks a strole fer de koolin' uv hiz mine, erwearin uv hiz nice cloes, an' feelin' lik a new man in de City Kounsil; de fust thing he know'd a lady glide up ter 'im an' put her han' lite on hiz arm. He jump 'roun' an' she say, mity flush'd up, "skuse me!'

"He see at wunst she er lady, but he wuz kinder lo' in
hiz sperrit, an' yit he wish in hiz hart dat she had gon ter
de udder en uv de rode, but he want ter hear her out.

"She tel 'im de site uv a man wuz medsin fer bad
eyes, dat nurly all uv 'em wuz cut down in de war an' dat
in konsquens it wuz er lonesum time fer wimmin; dey hev
nobody now ringin' de do' bells in de eebnin; no boys
sendin' 'em flowers an' 'fekshuns; no sweetarts tekin' 'em
walkin' on Sunday arternoons, an' weddins gwine out er
fashun. An' dis ain't de wust uv it. It mek us shamed. De
wives,--dey purrades 'roun' an' brags 'bout dere'ole mans'
an' cuts der eye at us skornful; an' de husban's iz mity
nigh es bad, erpokin' fun at us an' axin erbout de chillun.

"She say yer needn' think we're crazy ter marry;
tain't dat, an' tain't dat we want yer ter 'sport us,--no, no!
We hev money an' kin funnish our own vittuls an' cloes,
an' we kin wuk; but it iz dat reproach dey kas' on us, de
wear an' tear uv bein' laff'd at dat cuts us so deep. Ef I cud
be Mrs. Sumbody,--had sum proof dat I had de name uv
sum un,--sumthin' ter rub off de reproach. Dat's it,--dis
ding-dongin' uv de fokes at me.

"De man wuz pale es linnin, an' wuz hopin' ter ansur,
but fo' de wud floo frum his lips ernudder 'omun hooked
'im on de ter side. Mursy uv de Lord! two uv 'em had'im
an' it luk lik dey wuz gwine ter rip 'im in tew an' each tek
a haf. De las' wun tel her tale jes' lik de fust wun an' wuss.
She brung in tears es part uv her argurmint, an' de ter wun

got fretted an' used wuds dat wud hev konkurred 'im ef jes' den two mo',--two mo', mine yer, mekin' fo' in all, hed not kum up an' gits er grip on de gemmun, an' hiz eyes luk lik dey'd pop out his hed;--wun on each side an' two ter hiz face, an' it seems he gwine ter faint.

" 'Yer ladiz,' he says, 'may be rite in yer 'thuzasm, but yer iz too menny. Up ter dis time I hev bin shy uv wun, but ef I cud be erlowed ter choose jes' wun I mite try it.'

"Den de fo' wimmins begun ter git shaky wen a nur wun sailed in,--dat's five, den ernudder; dat's six, and den wun mo'--SEBUN!

"Luk, will yer! Sevun got wun man. It izn't sed wedder de wimmin wuz fer a partnurship wid de man es de kapertul, or wedder each uv 'em hoped ter beat out de udder six; but wun thing we know an' dat iz dat de po' man iz in de low grounds uv sorrur. Ter my min', de pikshur iz mity seerus, ebun do it mek us smile. Fur my

po' part, I iz glad we lives in fairer times. In our day mens iz awful plen'ful wid us, tho' I kin not say dat de qualty iz fust class in ve'y menny. But I thanks de Lord dat mos' enny nice leddy kin git merrid in dese times ef dey choose, an' dat wid out gwine out sparkin' fur de man. I notis dat ef she stay ter home, ten her buznis, min' her mudder, an' not sweep de streets too off'n wid her skirts, in de long run her modes' sperrit will win de day. I ubsurv ernudder thing; de unmerrid lady, de ole maid es sum calls her,--need not hang her haid. Jes' let her be quiet an' surv de Lord; jes' not fret 'bout wat fools says,--dey duz er heep uv talkin', but it iz lik de cracklin' uv de burnin' sticks under de pot, a big fuss an' a littul heat. Fer my part, I honners de 'oman dat b'haves hersef, briduls her tongue, duz her wuk, an' sings es she goes erlong. Her contentid sperrit beats a lazy husbun' ebry time, an' mity off'n it brings er gud husbun' erlong.

"Es fer dese fokes dat flurts an' skouts at ole maids dey ain' fitten ter live, an' ort ter be in de bottum uv Jeems Rivur, 'cept'n' dey'd spile de watur. No gemmun nur no lady wud do it.

"Now dis iz my wud 'bout de wimmin, an' I hope yer lik it, but if yer doant, jes' 'member dat Jasper sed it, an' will stan' by it, til de cows in de lo'er feil' kums home."

X
JASPER GLIMPSED UNDER VARIOUS LIGHTS

JASPER'S mother was near the century line when she died, and he attained unto the extraordinary age of eighty-nine. Truly there must have been rare endurance in the texture of the stock. Jasper's thoughts did not turn to religion until he was twenty-seven and yet by reason of his longevity he was a preacher for sixty years. During twenty-five years of that time he was a slave, and he had about thirty-five years of personal civil freedom, during which he won the distinctions that will make him a figure slow to pass out of history.

Jasper can have no successor. Freedom did not change him. It came too late for him to be seriously affected by its transforming hand. It never dazzled him by its festive charms nor crooked him with prejudice against the white people. There was far more for him in the traditions, sentiments, and habits of his bondage-days than in the new things which emancipation offered. He never took up with gaudy displays which marked his race in the morning of their freedom. This was especially true as to his ministry. He clung without apology to the old ways. In preaching, he spurned the new pulpit manners, the new style of dress, and all newfangrled tricks, which so fascinated his race. He intoned his sermons,--at least, in their more tender passages--sang the old revival songs of the plantations and factories, and felt it a part of his religion to smash, with giant hand, the innovations which the new order was bringing in. Of all the men whom I have known this weird, indescribable man cared the least for opposition;--unless he believed it touched his personal honour or was likely to injure the cause of religion. Indeed, he liked it. He was a born fighter and a stranger to fear. There was a charm in his resentments: they were of a high order, and inevitably commanded manly sympathy. He instinctively identified himself with the Lord and felt that when he fought he was fighting the Lord's battles. Satire and sarcasm were like Toledo blades in his hands. He often softened his attacks upon his enemies by such ludicrous hits and provoking jests that you felt that, after all, his hostility lacked the roots of hatred. He was far more prone to despise than to hate his enemies.

There is a curious fact in connection with Jasper's language Evidently in his early days his speech was atrociously ungrammatical. His dialect, while possessing an element of fascination, was almost unspellable. During his long ministerial life his reading and contact with educated people rooted out many of his linguistic excrescences. There were times when he spoke with approximate accuracy, and even with elegance; and yet he delighted, if indeed he was conscious of it, in returning to his dialect and in pouring it forth unblushingly in its worst shape, and yet always with telling effect. But the wonder of his speaking was his practical independence of language. When he became thoroughly impassioned and his face lit with the orator's glory, he seemed to mount above the bondage of words: his feet, his eyes, indeed every feature of his outer being became to him a new language. If he used words, you did not notice it. You were simply entranced and borne along on the mountain-tide of his passion. You saw nothing but him. You heard *him*; you felt him, and the glow of his soul was language enough to bring to you his message. It ought to be added that no man ever used the pause more eloquently or effectively than Jasper, and his smile was logic; it was rhetoric; it was blissful conviction.

Those who thought that Jasper was a mere raver did not know. Logic was his tower of strength. He never heard of a syllogism, but he had a way of marshalling his facts and texts which set forth his view as clear as the beaming sun. The Bible was to him the source of all authority, while his belief in the justice and truth of God was something unworldly. He understood well enough his frailties, his fallibility, and the tendency of the human soul towards unfairness and deceit. I heard him say once with irresistible effect: "Brutherin, Gord never lies; He can't lie. Men lie. I lie sometimes, I am very sorry to say it. I oughtn't to lie, and it hurts me when I do. I am tryin' ter git ober it, and I think I will by Gord's grace, but de Lord nevur lies." His tone in saying this was so humble and candid that I am sure the people loved him and believed in him more for what he said. A hypocrite could never have said it. Jasper could never be put into words. As he could speak without words so it is true that words could never contain him,--never tell his matchless story, never make those who did not hear him and see him fully understand the man that he was.

A notable and pathetic episode in Jasper's history was the fact that during the bitter days of the Confederacy when Richmond was crowded with hospitals,--hospitals themselves crowded with the suffering,--Jasper used to go in and preach to them. It was no idle entertainment provided by a grotesque player. He always had a message for the sorrowful. There is no extended record of his labours in the hospitals, but the simple fact is that he, a negro labourer with rude speech, was welcomed by these sufferers and heard with undying interest; no wonder they liked him. His songs were so mellow, so tender, so reminiscent of the southern plantation and of the homes from which these men came. His sermons had the ring of the old gospel preaching so common in the South. He had caught his manner of preaching from the white preachers and they too had been his only theological teachers. We can easily understand how his genius, seasoned with religious reverence, made him a winsome figure to the men who languished through the weary days on the cots. It cannot be said too often that Jasper was the white man's preacher. Wherever he went, the Anglo-Saxon waived all racial prejudices and drank the truth in as it poured in crystal streams from his lips.

Quite a pretty story is told of Jasper at the beginnings of his ministry. It seems that he went down into the eastern part of his town one Sunday to preach and some boisterous ruffians interfered, declaring that a negro had no right to go into the pulpit and that they would not allow Jasper to preach. A sailor who chanced to be present and knew Jasper faced these disorderly men and declared to them that Jasper was the smartest man in Virginia and that if he could take him to the country from whence he had come he would be treated with honour and distinction. There was also a small white boy standing by, and touched by the sincerity and power of Jasper, he pluckily jumped into the scene and exclaimed, "Yes, let him go on; what he says is all right. I have read it all in the Bible, and why shouldn't he speak?" The incipient mob was dispersed, and his audience was fringed with a multitude of white people who were attracted to the scene.

It is not intended by these things said, concerning Jasper's favour with the white people, to indicate that Jasper, in the least degree, was not with his own, race. Far from that. He loved his own people and was thoroughly identified with them; but he was larger than his race. He loved all men. He had grown up with that pleasing pride that the coloured people who lived in prominent families had about white people. Then, too, he had always been a man who had won favour wherever he went, and the white race had always had a respect and affection for him. Jasper was never ungrateful.

There were sometimes hard passages in the road which Jasper travelled. At the end of the war he was left high and dry, like driftwood on the shore. He had no church; no place to preach; no occupation. His relations with the white race were shattered, and things were grim enough; but ill-fortune could not break him. A large part of Richmond was in ashes, and in some places at least the work of rebuilding commenced at once,--or rather a clearing off of the debris with a view to rebuilding. Jasper walked out and engaged himself to clean bricks. During the Egyptian bondage the Hebrews made bricks and thought they had a hard lot; but Jasper spent the first days of his freedom in the brick business,--a transient expedient for keeping soul and body together until he could get on his feet again. Little thought the eager men who were trying to lay the foundations for their future fortunes that in the tall serious negro who sat whacking hour after hour at the bricks was one of God's intellectual noblemen. Born in bondage, lowly in his liberty and yet great in the gifts with which God had endowed him, it was Jasper's nature to be almost as cheerful when squatted on a pile of bricks and tugging at their cleaning as if he had a seat in a palace and was feeding on royal dainties. He carried the contented spirit, and that too while he aspired after the highest. He did not uselessly kick against the inevitable, but he always strove for the best that was in his reach.

One of the most serious jars of Jasper's life was his conflict with some of his brethren in connection with his notable and regrettable sermon on the motion of the sun. Intelligent people do not need to be told that Jasper knew nothing of natural science, and that his venture into the field of astronomy was a blunder. It was a matter that did not in the least involve his piety or his salvation, nor even his ministerial efficiency. His whole bearing in the matter was so evidently sincere, and his respect for the Bible, as he understood it, was so unmeasured that it set him off rather to an advantage than to a disadvantage. It is told in another place how he was drawn into the preaching of that sermon which gave him an odd, and yet a genuine, celebrity. It was no love for sensation and no attempt to show his learning, but simply an attempt to vindicate the Bible as he understood it. When the sermon was first delivered it created a wide-spread sensation. Some of the coloured ministers of Richmond were shocked out of their equanimity, and they felt that something must be done. It was a case of hysterics. In a fit of freakish courage some of them made an attack on Jasper. A letter was written to a Richmond paper and signed by several prominent negro Baptists, one of them being the pastor of a strong church. In this letter Jasper's sermons were bitterly denounced, and they were spoken of as "a base fabrication," out of time and place, and doing more harm than good. It was said further that these sermons had drawn such crowds that it had resulted in the injury of a number of persons, and that a better way for the author of these sermons would be for him to preach Jesus Christ and Him crucified.

Some time after this the Ebenezer Baptist Church called a conference to consider the situation and to see if matters could not be adjusted. Jasper was an ardent believer in the independence of the individual Baptist church, and he was summoned to appear before that conference. He refused to go, saying that he did not recognize the authority of the church to interfere with him. Thereupon they sent a committee to him inviting him to come and make any statement that he wished to make concerning the question at issue.

He went. The point in the published letter concerning Jasper that was most offensive to him was the statement as to "base fabrication." That hit him between the joints of the harness. His soul was stirred with a furious resentment, and when he got before that council and fell afoul of the three men who had charged him with "a base fabrication" it was a day not to be forgotten. When he had got through it would be hard to say how many baskets would have been required to hold the fragments. The man who had really written the letter suddenly discovered that it had no reference on the earth to Brothel Jasper. It was intended to answer something that had been said in a paper in New York. Attempts were made to refresh his memory. Quite a respectable minister reminded this letter writer that they had talked together concerning this letter, and that the attention of the writer was called to the "base fabrication" part of it, but the memory of the brother could not be revived. No stimulant could reach the case. Other folks might charge Brother

Jasper with base fabrication, but not this man. It was a lamentable and discreditable conclusion. He was crippled in both feet and respected by none. This ended the matter. Jasper strode away from the council with the marks of victory about him; and while bad feeling could not die at once, yet the attacks on Jasper went entirely out of fashion. Let it be added that there were multitudes who shared the prejudice against this old warrior, but little cared he. On he went his fine way, growing in nobleness, and loving the God in whom he believed.

Jasper's pleasures were of the meditative sort. For a long time his church gave him an ample vacation in the summer. He retired to the country and courted its quiet. His only sport was fishing along the streams, and that suited his task. If the fish didn't bite, his thoughts always did. Like the fish they ran in schools, but unlike the fish they ran in all weathers and in all seasons. But Jasper never achieved marked success in the art of recreation. Go where he might, his fame was there to confront and to entangle him.

Demands for him to preach always came in hot and thick, and there was hardly a Sunday when Jasper was in the country that he was not surrounded by a crowd and preaching with everglowing fervour and delight. Indeed, Jasper was sought after to dedicate churches, deliver lectures and to preach special sermons in every part of Virginia, and often beyond it. It was said that he preached in almost every county and city in Virginia. He was the one ever sought Virginia preacher, and in that respect he stood unmatched by any man of his race.

As a rule, Jasper did not preach very long sermons. His Sunday afternoon sermons very rarely exceeded fifty minutes in length, but on extraordinary occasions he took no note of time. Jasper was not a sermon-maker. He did not write them, and homiletics was a thing of which he had never heard. He was fond of pictorial preaching and often selected historical topics, such as "Joseph and His Brethren" or "Daniel in the Lion's Den," or "The Raising of Lazarus." He had quite a large stock of special sermons,--sermons which had grown by special use, and which embodied the choicest creations of his mind. These he preached over and over again and in his own pulpit, and without apology to anybody. But after all the themes which interested him most profoundly and on which he preached with unsurpassed ardour and rapture were the fundamental doctrines of the Scriptures. The last sermon he ever preached was on Regeneration; and on many phases of the Christian system he preached with consummate ability. He believed fully in the doctrine of future punishment, and his description of the fate of the lost made the unbelieving quake with terror and consternation. His preaching was of that fervid, startling, and threatening sort, well suited to awaken religious anxieties and to bring the people to a public confession. He was his own evangelist,--did chiefly the work of bringing his congregation to repentance, and the growth of his church consisted almost entirely of the fruit of his own ministry. His church on the island began with nine members, and it was reported that there were over 2,000 at the time of his death. He had uncommon caution about receiving people into his church. He was not willing to take people to count, and he preached searchingly to those who were thinking of applying for membership.

Just two little and yet important things call for a place in this chapter. Jasper was an inexorable debt-payer. The only debt that he could tolerate was a church debt, and he could ill tolerate that. The unsettled account of his great new church building grappled him like a nightmare. It was his burden in the day and his torturing dream at night. Even during his dying days the church debt haunted and depressed him, and loud among his parting exhortations was his insistent plea that the church debt should be speedily paid.

In his early life Jasper contracted the use of tobacco,--as, indeed, almost his entire race did, and he was also quite free with the use of alcoholic drinks,--though never, so far as is known, to the extent of intoxication. No question as to his sobriety has ever ridden the air. But these habits lingered with him long after he entered the ministry, and even until he was winning enviable and far-spreading favour as a preacher. So far as known, these facts did not becloud his reputation nor interfere with his work. Of course, he never entered a barroom, and never drank convivially, but he kept liquor in his house, and took it as his choice dictated. But gradually it worked itself into his conscience that these things were not for the best, and without the least ostentation or even publicity he absolutely abandoned the use both of tobacco and alcoholic drinks. He made no parade about it, and took on no fanatical airs. Just as he thought it was wrong to owe money which he could not pay and therefore hated a debt, so he felt that these habits, useless at best, might really be harmful to him and to others, and therefore he gave them up.

His moral and religious ideals were very lofty, and he lived up to them to a degree not true of

MONUMENT OVER JOHN JASPER'S GRAVE

MONUMENT OVER JOHN JASPER'S GRAVE

many. Not long after his death a really magnificent monument was erected over his grave. It was quite costly, and the money for it was raised by his church people and other lovers of whom he had legions. While he lived, legislators, judges, governors, and many men of eminent distinction, went to hear him preach. Many of the most distinguished white ministers of the country made it a point to go to his church on Sunday afternoon whenever they were in the city, and he was justly ranked as one of the attractions of Richmond.

Now that he has found his grave not far from the site of his church, and this stately shaft has been placed as a sentinel over his dust, multitudes as they come and go will visit the tomb of the most original, masterful, and powerful negro preacher of the old sort that this country has ever produced.

XI
SERMON:--THE STONE CUT OUT OF THE MOUNTAIN
(*Text, Daniel 2:45.*)

THIS rugged specimen of historical eloquence constituted the sermon delivered on Sunday afternoon, July 20, 1884. Jasper mounted the pulpit with the dash of an athlete and tripped around the platform during the preliminaries with the air of a racer. A sense of strength imparted to his face the triumphant glow. A smile parted his lips, and told the secret of an animated and aggressive courage.

"I stan's befo' you to-day on legs of iron and nun kin stay me from preachin' de Gospil uv de Lord Gord. I know well nuff dat de ole devul is mad as a tempest 'bout my bein' here; he knows dat my call ter preach kums frurn Gord, and dat's wat meks 'im so mad wen he sees Jasper 'scend de pulpit, fur he knows dat de people is gwine ter hear a messige straight frum heaven. I don't git my sermuns out uv grammars an' reterricks, but de Sperrit uv de Lord puts 'em in my mind an' meks 'em burn in my soul."

His manner was radiant, courageous, defiant, and was prophetic of one of his greatest discourses.

"It hev always bin one uv de ways uv Gord ter set up men as rulers uv de people. Yer know dat Gord ordains

kings and rulers an',--wat kinder bodders sum uv us,--He
don't always mek it a p'int ter put up good men. Yer know
dat our Lord giv Judis a place 'mong de twelve, an' he
turn'd out ter be one uv de grandes' raskils under de sun.

"Jes' so Nebukidnezzur was pinted uv de Lord ter be
king uv Babylon,--dat same robbur dat tuk de vessuls out
uv de temple at Jerusalem an' lugged 'em away ter his
own country. Dat man had wun uv de powerfullest
kingdums evur known on dis flat earth. He ruled over
many countries and many smaller kingdums, an' even had
under his hands de servunts on de plantashun an' de beasts
uv de feil'. He was one uv dese unlimertid monnuks. He
axed nobody no odds, an' did jes' wat he wanted ter do,
an' I kinnot stop ter tell yer wid wat a strong hand an'
outstretched arm he ruled de people wid an irun rod. It
kum ter pass dat one time dis king dat did not fear Gord
(tho' Gord had sot him up), had a dream. Dreams iz
awfully curus things. Dey used ter frighten folks out'n
dere senses an' I tell yer dey sometimes frighten folks
now. I've had many dreams in my day dat got mity close
ter me. Dey gravuled inter de very

cords uv my soul, an' made me feel lik de groun' under
my feet wuz libul ter giv way any time, an' I don't dout
dat hundreds uv yer dat hear me now hev bin frightened
an' cud not eat nor sleep nor wuk wid any peace 'caus' yer
done hev strange dreams. Yer better watch dem dreams.
In de anshient days de Lord spoke ter folks in dreams. He

warned dem, an' I don't dout dat He duz dat way sometimes now.

"Neberkidnezzur's dream stirred him powerful. He rolled all night an' did not sleep a wink. So he sent out an'got de magishuns an' de strolgurs an' de sorserers an' de Kaldeuns, an' dey wuz brought unter him. He tell 'em dat he had dreamed a dream dat had trubbled his sperrit. An' de Kaldeuns axed him wat de dream wuz. De king say dat de dream done gone clear out'n him, an' he can't cotch de straight uv it ter save his soul. He tell 'em, moreovur, dat dey got ter dig up de dream an' work up de meanin' too, an' dat ef dey don't dat he gwine ter have 'em cut all ter pieces an' turn dere houses inter a dunghill, an' den he tell 'em dat ef dey will git de dream back fur him an' give de explernashun he gwine ter give 'em nice gifs an' put gret honurs on 'em. It waz too much fer de Kaldeuns. Dey cudn't dream de king's dream fer 'im, an' dey kum squar out an' tell Nebukidnezzur dat no man on de earth cud show sich a matter ter de king, an' dat in dere erpinyun dar is no king on de earth dat wud ax fer sich a thing frum proffit or magishun.

"Den Nebukidnezzur got high. He went on a tare an' yer know wen a king gits mad yer better git out er his way. He is got de power; an' so he up an' sent out a decree through all de regiuns uv de kingdom dat all de wise men everywhar shud be slain. Jes' see wat a mad man will do wen he git furius mad. Dey got no mo' sens dan a mad tiger or a roarin' lion. Jes' befo' de slaughter uv de wise men kum on, Daniel hear 'bout it, an' he axed de king's captin wat it wuz all 'bout an' why de king wuz so hasty, an' de captin tol' Dan'l all 'bout it. Dan'l brushed hissef up quick and struck out to see de king an' ax him ter hol' up de exercushun uv his bloody profesy, an' he'd promise to splain his dream ter him. Den Dan'l goes off an' gits all his Godly frien's togedder an' ax 'em ter pray ter de Gord uv heaven dat he an' his frien's shud not perish in de slaughter uv de tricksters uv dat country. One thing de Lord can't do;--He can't refuse ter answer de cries uv His people; an' wen all dat prayin' wuz gwine on Gord appeared to Dan'l in de nite an' revealed ter him de secret uv de king,--an' wat yer reckin? Wen de Lord giv Dan'l dat dream an' de hinterpertashun dar of, Dan'l raised a gret shout an' giv thanks to Gord for wat de Lord had done fer him. But he didn't shout long, fer he had important bisnis ter attend ter; an' very soon he went ter de king an' kerried wid him de secrit dat de king had demandid at de han's uv de erstrolgers an' magishuns. He told de king rite ter his face de thing dat he had dreamed, an' wat Gord meant by it. Truly Dan'l did behave hissef befo' de king in a very pretty an' becomin' manner. He tel de king he did not hav no mo sens dan udder people, an' dat he wuz not perpar'd to do things dat udder men cud do, but dat it wuz by de power uv Gord dat all dis matter had bin made known ter him. He tol' de king dat wat he saw wuz a gret imige; dat de imige wuz brite an splendid an' de form uv it wuz terrerbul; dat de hed wuz uv fine gold, his brest and arms uv silvur, his belly an' thize uv brass, an' his legs uv irun and his feet part uv irun an' part uv clay. An' he tel de king fudder dat he saw er stone dat wuz cut widout han's out'n de mountin an' dat de stone smote de imige erpun his feet an' broke 'em in pieces, an' dat de stone dat brok de imige became a gret mountin an' filled all de wurl'. Den Dan'l,--dat brave an' feerles bruther, dat nevur quailed befo' de mitiest ruler uv de earth,--faced de king an' tel 'im an orful an' a warnin' troof. He say ter 'im, 'Yer is a gret king now. Yer hav er mity country an' all power, an' thy glory civers de groun'. Man an' beas' an' foul obey yer. Yer iz de hed uv gold, but arter yer will kum anudder kingdum dat shall not be lik yourn, but still it shal be big an' dar shall kum anudder kingdum and dar shall be a fo'th kingdom strong as irun, an' dis kingdum shall brooz an' smash all de udder kingdums.'

"An' den Dan'l gits ter de big pint. He tels de king dat de Lord is gwine ter set up er kingdum an' dat in de times ter kum dat kingdum shall crush an' cornsume all de udder kingdums. Dat shall be de kingdum uv Gord on de earth, an' dat kingdum shall stan' fer evur an' evur. You knows how yer saw de stone dat wuz cut out'n de mountin an' how dat broke in pieces de irun, de bras, de clay, de silvur, an' de gold, an' my Gord hev made known ter you, O king, wat shall tek place in de gret herearter, and dis is de dream an' de hinterpertashun dar of.

"Dat wuz a mity sermon dat Dan'l preached ter Nebukidnezzur. It ort ter hev saved 'im, but it look lik it med 'im wuss. De debbul got 'im fer dat time an' he turn rite agin de Lord Gord an' sot at nort His stashutes an' countid His ways onholy.

"Yer know 'bout dat imige. It wuz med uv gold, an' wuz threescore cubits high and six cubits wide, an' twuz sot up in de plain uv Durer, not fer frum Bablun. Yer know er cubit is about eighteen inchis, an' ef yer multerply dat by threescore cubits yer git 1080 inches, wich mean dat de imige wuz ninety foot high an' nine feet broad. So yer see Nebukidnezzur got ter be a Gordmakur, an' wen he got dis gret imige bilt he sont out ter git all de princis an' guvnurs an' all de res' uv de swell folks ter kum an' bow down an' wurshep dat gret imige dat he had sot up. Now dis wuz de gret folly an' shame uv de king. By dat deed he defied de Lord Gord an' de raff uv de Lord wuz stirr'd agin 'im.

"An' now, my brudderin, yer member Dan'l tol' de king dat de imige dat he saw in his dream wuz 'imsef rulin' over all de udder kingdums. He tol' 'im also dat dat stone dat wuz cut out uv de mountin an' kum rollin' down de craggy sides an' broke in pieces de irun, de brass an' de clay, dat dat wuz de kingdum uv de Lord Jesus Christ. An' he tel 'im, fuddermo, dat de kummin' uv de stone ter be a great mountin means de growth uv de kingdum uv our Lord tel it shall fil dis wurl' an' shall triumf over all de udder kingdums. Dan'l tel de king dat his kingdum wuz gwine ter be taken frum him, 'caus' he had not feared de Gord uv heaven, an' in his folly an' crimes he turned away

113

frum dat Gord dat rules in de heaven an' hols de nashuns uv de earth in de pams uv His han's. He tol' 'im dat de kingdum uv Satun, dat arch ennimy uv Gord, wuz gwine ter tumbul flat, 'caus' dat stone cut out uv de mountin wud roll over Satun's derminyuns an' crush it in ter flinders.

"Glory ter Gord in de highis'; dat stone cut out uv de mountin is a mity roller. Nuthin kin stay its terribul progris! Dey dat fite erginst Jerhover had bettur look out,--dat stone is still rollin' an' de fust thing dey know it will crush down erpon 'em an' dey will sink ter rise no mo'. Our Gord is er cornsumin' fire, an' He will overturn an' overturn tel de foundashuns uv sin iz brokin up. Yer jes' wait er little. De time is fas' rollin' on. Evun now I hear my Saviour sayin' ter His Father, 'Father, I kin stay here no longer; I mus' git up dis mornin'; I am gwine out ter call My people frum de feil'; dey hav ben abused and laughed at an' bin med a scoffin' long nuff fer My name's sake. I kin stay no longer. My soul cries fer My chillun. Gabrul, git down yer trumpit dis mornin'; I want yer ter do some blowin'. Blow gently an' easy at fust, but let My people hear your goldin notes. Dey will kum wen I call.'

"Ah, my brutherin, you an' I wil be dar wen dat trumpit soun's. I don' think I shall be erlarm'd, 'caus' I shall know it iz my king marshallin' His people home. It won't frighten you my sisters; it will hev de sweetnis uv Jesus vois ter yer; an', oh, how it will ring out dat happy mornin' wen our king shall kum to gather de ransomed uv de Lord ter 'imsef. Den yer shall hev a new an' holy body, an' wid it your glorified sperrit shall be united, an' on dat day we shall go in ter see de Father an' He shall smile an' say: 'Dese iz My chillun; dey hav washed dere robes and made dem white in de blood uv de Lamb; dey hav kum out uv gret tribberlashun an' dey shall be wid Me for ever an' ever.' I speck ter be dar.

"'Well, Jasper,' yer say, 'why yer spec ter be dar. How yer know?' Yer read de foteenth chapter uv John, will yer? 'I go ter prepar er place fer yer,' an' dat word is ter rule; an' so yer will see ole John Jasper rite dar, an' King Jesus shall kum out ter meet us an' tek us in an' sho' us de manshuns dat He hav prepared fer us.

"O Lusifer how thou hav fallin! You proud ones will find den dat your days iz over, an' ye dat hav despised de chillun uv my Gord wil sink down inter hell, jes' as low es it is posserbul ter git. Yer needn't tel 'im dat yer hev preached in His name, an' in His name done many wonderful works. Yer can't fool Him! He'll frown down at yer an' say: I don't know yer, an' I don't wan ter know yer, an' I don' wan ter see yer. Git out uv My site forever, an' go ter your place ermong de lost.

"Ah, truly, it is a mity stone, bin rollin' all dese senshuriz, rollin' to-day. May it roll through the kingdum uv darknis and crush de enemis uv Gord. Dat stone done got so big dat it is higher dan heav'n, broader dan de earth, and deeper dan hell hitsef. But don't be deceived.

Don't think dat I don' let yer off. I got somethin' more fer yer yit.

"Yer member Dan'l and Shadrick, Meeshick an' Erbedniggo. Dey all stubbonly fused to bow down ter Nebukidnezzur's golden imige. Dey stood straight up. Dey wudn't bend a knee nor cruk a toe, an' dem Kaldeeuns wuz waatchin' um. Dat's de way hit always iz; de debbul's folks iz always er watchin' us an' tryin' ter git sumthin' on us an' ter git us inter trubbul an' wid too many uv us dey succeed. Dey saw dat Dan'l an' his friens wud not git down lik dey dun, an' up dey jumped an' away dey cut an' kum ter de king.

" 'Oh, king, liv ferevur,' dey say. 'Yer know, O king, wat yer sed,--dat dercree dat yer made. dat at de soun' uv de kornit, de flute, de harp, de sackbut, de saltry an' de dulsermur an' orl kines uv musik, dat ev'ry body shud fall down an' wurshep de goldin imige, an' dat dose dat duz not fall down an' worshep shud be put in de furnis; an' now, oh, king, dey say dat a lot uv dose men dun refews. Dey doan regard yer. Dey hate yer Gods an' spize de imige dat yer sot up.'

"Coarse de ole king got mad agin an' in his fury dey brought dese three befo' him. He axed um ef wat he had heerd 'bout um wuz so,--'bout dere not worsheppin' de goldin imige. 'Mayby yer med a mistake,' de king say, 'but we gwine ter hev it ovur agin, an' ef wen de ban' strikes up nex' time yer will git down an' worshop it'll go eezy wid yer, an' ef yer doant de fires in de furnis will be startid quick es litenin' an' inter it ev'ry one uv yer shall go.'

"Dese wuz yung men, but, ah, I tel yer, dey wuz uv de loyul stock. Dey wuz jes' es kam es sunrise in de mornin'. Dey sed: 'Oh, king, we ain' keerful ter anser 'bout dis mattur. Ef yer lik ter cas' us inter de furnis, our Gord dat we surv iz abul ter git us out. We ain' gwine ter bow, an' we nevur will bow ter your Gord, an' yer jes' es well understan'.'

"Rite den de men wont ter heet up de furnis. Dey wuz tol' ter heet it up sevun times hottur dan wuz de ginrul rule an' dey hed sum jiunts ter tie Shedrak, Meeshik, an' Erbedniggo, an' dey tuk de yung men away inter de furnis. De heet wuz so terribul dat de flames shot out an' sot fire ter de men dat had put de Hebru chillun in an' de po' retchiz wuz burn'd up, but not a hair uv de three yung men wuz sing'd, an' dey kum out er smilin' an' not a blistur on um frum hed ter fut. Dey did not evun hev any smell uv fire 'bout dere pussuns, an' dey luk jes' lik dey jes' kum out uv dressin' rums.

"Neberkidnezzur wuz dar, an' he say: 'Luk in dat furnis dar. We didn't put but three pussons in dar, did we?' an' dey tol' 'im dat wuz so. Den he tun pale an' luk skeered lik he gwine ter die an' he say:

" 'Luk dar; I see fo' men inside an' walkin' through de fire, an' de form uv de fourth is lik de Son uv Gord,' an' it luk lik de king got kunvurtid dat day, fur he lif' up his vois an' shout de praiz uv de Gord uv Shedrak, Meeshik an' Erbedniggo.

"Ah, gret iz dis story; dey dat trus' in Gord shall nevur be put ter kornfushun. De righteous alwaz kums out konkerurs an' more dan konkerurs. Kings may hate yer, frien's spize yer, an' cowurds bakbite yer, but Gord iz yer durlivrur.

"But I dun forgit. Dis ole time rerlijun iz not gud nuff fer sum folks in dese las' days. Sum call dis kine uv talk foolishnis, but hif dat be troo den de Bibul, an' hevun, an' dese Christun's hearts, iz ful uv dat kine uv foolishnis. Ef dis be ole fogy rerlijun, den I want my church crowdid wid ole fogiz.

"Wat did John see ober dar in Patmos? He say he saw de fo' an' twenty eldurs seatid roun' de throne uv Gord an' castin' dere glittrin' crowns uv gold at de feet uv King Jesus, an' he say dat out uv de throne kum lightnin' an' thundurs an' voicis an' de sevun lamps burnin' befo' de throne uv Gord. An' dar befo' de throne wuz de sea uv glass, an' roun' 'bout de throne wuz de fo' livin' creaturs ful uv eyes befo' an' behine, an' dey nevur ceas cryin': 'Holy, Holy, Holy, iz de Lord Gord almity dat died ter tek away de sins uv de wurl'!'"

"Yer call dat ole fogy. Jes' luk away ober yondur in de future. Duz yer see dat sea uv glass an' de saints uv Gord dat wuz all bruised an' mangul'd by de fi'ry darts uv de wickid. I hear um singin'! Wat iz dere song? Oh, how it rolls! an' de korus iz: 'Redeemed, redeemed, wash'd in de blud uv de Lam'. Call dem ole fogiz, do yer? Wel yer may, fer dey iz bin doin' dat way frum de time dat Abel, de fust man, a saved soul told de news uv salvashun ter de anjuls.

" 'Wel, Jasper, hev yer got any rerlijun ter giv way?'

"I'se free ter say dat I ain't got es much es I want. Fur forty-five years I bin beggin' fur mo', an' I ax fur mo' in dis tryin' hour. But, bless Gord, I's got rerlijun ter giv way. De Lord hev fil'd my hands wid de Gorspil, an' I stan' here ter offur free salvashun ter any dat wil kum. Ef in dis big crowd dar iz one lost sinnur dat hev not felt de klinsin' tech uv my Saviur's blud, I am 'im ter kum terday an' he shall nevur die."

XII
FACTS CONCERNING THE SERMON ON THE SUN

LET me say in frankness that when I originally began this appreciation of John Jasper it was my full purpose to omit from it all reference to his very notorious sermon on "The Sun Do Move." That was the one thing in his life I most regretted--an episode that I was quite willing to commit to oblivion. I felt that it was a distinct discredit to him. But upon further reflection I have concluded that the omission might hurt him far more than the facts in the case possibly could. Inasmuch also as it was that very sermon which drew to him such widespread attention, and since there are those who never heard him, nor heard of him except in connection with that sermon, I have decided to give the public the facts in the case and the sermon itself. In this chapter I will give a history of the sermon, and in the next I will give the substance of the sermon. It is due to my old friend and brother, Jasper, to say that he really never intended to create a sensation by preaching on an exciting or unusual topic. This he most solemnly declared, and while he was several sensations himself in a single bunch, and while almost every sermon that he preached produced wild and thrilling sensations, he did not work for that. He started his chief sensations by preaching the Gospel in such a hot, pungent, and overmastering way that his people could not contain themselves. Jasper tells us how it all came about. Two of his brethren, members of his flock, fell into a friendly dispute as to whether the sun did revolve around the earth or not. As they could not decide the question, and neither would yield, they finally agreed to submit the question to their old pastor, solemnly believing, I dare say, that there was no mystery in earth, sea, or sky that he could not fathom.

When Jasper's theme went abroad it called forth some very scornful criticisms from one of his Baptist neighbours--one of the "eddicatid preachers," as Jasper delighted to call them, though in certain moods he often finished his sentence by branding them as eddicatid fools. When he heard of the strictures mentioned above, he let fly some shot at white heat as a response to the attacks on him. When he got a thing in his blood the amenities of controversy sometimes lost their place in his memory. He would let fly flings of satire that would be toothsome topics for street gossip for many summer Sundays. Things for zestful chat rarely ran short when Jasper was about. He expressed much regret that he had come in conflict with the "furlosofurs" of the day, freely confessing his ignorance in the matter of "book-larnin'." His knowledge, he said, was limited to the Bible, and much of that he did not feel that he could explain. But on the question about the sun he was sure that he possessed the true light. "I knows de way uv de sun, as de Wurd of Gord tells me," he declared in his warlike manner, "an' ef I don' pruv' dat de sun moves den yer may pos' me as er lier on ev'ry street in Richmun'." By this time his war paint was plainly visible, and his noble defiance rang out like a battle call.

The occasion on which I heard his "astronomical sermon," as one of his opponents deridingly dubbed it, was not at its first presentation. He had delivered it repeatedly before and knew his ground. The gleam of confidence and victory shone clear and strong on his face.

The audience looked like a small nation. Long before the solemn janitor, proud of his place, strict to the minute, swung open the front doors, the adjacent streets swarmed with the eager throngs. Instantly there was a rush, and in surged the people, each anxious to get a seat. The spacious house was utterly inadequate to the exigencies of the hour. Many crowded the aisles, disposed themselves around the pulpit, sat on pew-arms, or in friendly laps.

Jasper's entrance was quite picturesque. He appeared in the long aisle weaxing a cape overcoat, with a beaver in one hand, and his cane in the other, and with a dignity not entirely unconscious. His officers rose to welcome him, one removing his great coat, another his head piece, and yet another his cane. As he ascended the pulpit he turned and waved a happy greeting to his charge and it fairly set his emotional constituents to shouting. Many loving words were said out in a rattling chorus in token of their happiness at seeing him.

It is more than probable that some of Jasper's young people had notions of their own as to his views of the sun; but never a word would they let slip that could mortify their beloved old pastor, or give a whisper of comfort to his critics. They were for Jasper, and the sun might go its way. They believed in their pastor, believed in his goodness, his honesty, and his greatness.

In the opening exercises there occurred several characteristic incidents. He requested his choir to open by singing, "The Heavens Declare the Glory of God." This was at once a proof of his seriousness and of his sense of the fitting.

When he arose to read the Scriptures, he glanced around at his audience, and bowing in pleased recognition of the many white people present, he said with unaffected modesty that he hoped that the "kin' frens who'd come ter hur me would 'scuse my urrors in readin'. My eyes is gitting weak an' dim, and I'se slow in making out de hard wurds." Then he proceeded with utmost reverence to read the passage selected for the service. He was not a good reader, but there was a sobriety and humility in his manner of reading the Scriptures that made one always feel a peculiar respect for him.

There may be place here for a passing word about this most original and picturesque representative of his race. Jasper had a respect for himself that was simply tremendous. Unconsciously he carried a lofty crest, and yet you knew there was no silly conceit in it. His walk along the street was not that of a little man who thought all eyes were upon him, but of a giant who would hide from himself and from others the evidences of his power. His conversation carried an assertion of seriousness--his tones were full of dignity--his bearing seemed to forbid any unseemly freedom--and in public you saw at once that he was holding himself up to a high standard. Of course, when he was in the high frenzy of public speech and towering to his finest heights he lost the sense of himself, but he was then riding the wind and cleaving the sky and no rules made by men could apply to him. But along with self-appreciation,--always one of his attractions to me,--was a noble and delicate respect for others. He loved his own people, and they lived in the pride of it, but he had a peculiarly hospitable and winsome attitude towards strangers. He was quite free in his cordiality towards men, and I delighted to see how my coming to hear him pleased him. In his off-hand way, he said to me one Sunday afternoon as he welcomed me to the pulpit: "Glad to see you; it does me good to have folks around whar got sense; it heps me ter preach better. Mighty tough to talk to folks whar ain' got no brains in de head."

He had a double consciousness that was always interesting to me. He was always full of solicitude about his sermon. It lay a burden on him, and it required no expert to discover it. He had so much sincerity that his heart told its secrets through his face. But think not that this made him oblivious to his surroundings. His heart was up towards the throne, and his soul was crying for strength, but his eye was open to the scene before him. The sight of the audience intoxicated him; the presence of notable people caught his gaze and gladdened him; tokens of appreciation cheered him, and he paid good price in the way of smiles and glances to those who showed that he was doing them good. It made a rare combination--his concern for his message, and his happy pride in his constituents. It gave a depth to his feeling and a height to his exultation. He swung between two great emotions and felt the enrichment of both.

The text for his sermon was a long cry from his topic. It was: "The Lord God is a man of war; The Lord is His name." He was too good a sermon-maker to announce a text and abandon it entirely, and so he roamed the Old Testament to gather illustrations of the all-conquering power of God. This took him over a half hour to develop, and as it took even much longer to formulate his argument as to the rotation of the sun it made his sermon not only incongruous, but intolerably long--far longer than any other sermon that I ever knew him to preach. The two parts of the discourse had no special kinship, while the first part tired the people before he reached the thing they came for. It was an error in judgment, but his power to entertain an audience went far to save him from the consequences of his mistake.

The intelligent reader will readily understand the drift of his contention about the sun. What he said, of course, was based on the literal statements of the Old Testament, written many centuries ago, not as a treatise on astronomy, but in language fitted to express ideas from the standpoint of the times in which it was used. Jasper knew of no later discoveries in the natural world, and, therefore, very sincerely believed with religious sincerity, and all the dogmatism of ignorance, that the declarations of the old Scriptures were true in very jot and tittle. It is apparent enough that to the enlightened people who went to hear the address merely for amusement there was rare fun in the whole performance. To them, Jasper was an ignorant old simpleton, a buffoon of the pulpit, a weakling to be laughed at. And yet hardly that. He was so dead in earnest, and withal so shrewd in stating his case, so quick in turning a point, and brimming with such choice humour and sometimes flashing out such keen, telling strokes of sarcasm, that he compelled the admiration of his coldest critics. To the untutored people before him Jasper was the apostle of light. They believed every syllable that fell from his lips--he was the truth to them--they stood where other honest and godly people stood for ages and saw things just as they saw them. Their opinion as to the sun did not in the least affect their piety, for, as a fact, they believed just exactly as the grandfathers of Jasper's critics believed sixty years before.

It was worth while being there. Jasper was in his most flexible, masterful mood, and he stormed the heights with his forces in full array. At times, the negroes would be sending forth peals of laughter and shouting in wildest response, "Yas, Lord; dat's so, Brer Jasper; hit 'em ergin, bless God! Glory, glory, tell us more, ole man!" Then he would fly beyond the sun and give them a glimpse of the New Jerusalem, and they would be crying and bursting forth with snatches of song until you would think the end had come. But not so by ever so much. A word from Jasper would bring the stillness of death, and he would be the master again and ready for new flights.

When the excitement about the sermon was at its full blow, human greed, ever keen-scented, sensed money in Jasper and his sermon, and laid a scheme to trade on the old man and his message. A syndicate was formed to send him out as a lecturer, hoping that the Northern love for the negro, and the catchiness of the subject, would fill vast halls with crowds to hear the old man, and turn in rich revenues, of which they would reap the larger part.

Jasper, for reasons by no means mercenary, was tickled by this new turn in fortune. He was not wanting in the pride of successful ambition and this new proof of his growing distinction naturally pleased him. Fame was pinning her medals fast upon him, and he liked it. Not that he was infatuated with the notion of filling his private pocket. As a fact, he never uttered in my hearing one sentence that showed his love of money, or his eagerness to get it. But he was much wedded to the idea of a new house of worship for his people, and any proper method that would aid in bringing this happy consummation was joy to his generous old soul. His heart dwelt with his flock, and to honour and cheer them was life to him.

Of course, his church fell in with the idea. Anything to please "Brother Jasper" was the song of their lives. It looked wonderfully grand to them to see glory crowning their pastor and gold pouring in to build them a temple. It was with pomp and glee they sent him away. The day of his departure was celebrated with general excitement and with cheering groups at the train.

But in some way providence did not get identified with the new enterprise. The first half of his sermon was a trial to people set on sensation. The Lord in his military character did not appeal. Some actually retired after the first part, and an eclipse to hopes uncounted fell over the scene. Jasper, as a show, proved a failure, for which the devout may well give thanks. He got as far as Philadelphia, and even that historically languid city found life too brief and brisk to spend in listening for ninety-odd minutes to two uncongenial discourses loosely bundled into one. The old man had left the sweet inspiration of his demonstrative church in Richmond, and felt a chill of desolation when he set foot on alien soil. The tides of invisible seas fought against him, empty benches grinned at him, and he got homesick. The caravan collapsed, the outfit tumbled into anarchy, the syndicate picked up the stage clothes and stole out in the night-gloom, the undaunted but chagrined Jasper made a straight shoot for

Richmond; ever after the Jasper Lecture Bureau was a myth, without ancestry or posterity.

Think not that there was chill in the air when Jasper struck Richmond on his return. No word of censure awaited him. His steadfast adherents hailed him as a conqueror and his work went on. His enemies--an envious crop ever being on hand--tossed a few stones over the back fence, but Jasper had a keen relish for battle, and was finest when his foes were the fiercest. Antagonism gave zest to his dramatic career.

Permit the writer to slip in here a word as to Jasper's devotion to his old master, Mr. Samuel Hargrove. I knew Mr. Hargrove well. He was a man with a heart. I knew him as an old man while I was young. He had a suburban home near Manchester, his business and church were in Richmond. I often saw him in my congregation at the Bainbridge Street Baptist church, Manchester, and thus often met him. Shrinking, without public gifts, full of kindliness, and high in his life, he commanded the heart of his servant who to the last delighted to honour his memory. Their relations did not prevent their mutual respect and affection. The hideous dogma of social equality never thrust itself into their life. They had good-will and esteem one for the other, and lived together in peace. Jasper was a lover and admirer of white people, and delighted to serve and honour them, and in return the white people were fond of him and glad to help him.

I rejoice that this old minister, the quaint and stern veteran, came in God's time to a righteous fame. Public opinion is an eccentric and mysterious judge. It has an unarticulated code for fixing the rank and fate of mortals. It is a large and ill-sorted jury, and its decisions often bring surprise at the time, but they never get reversed. The jurymen may wrangle during the trial, but when it emerges from the council room and renders the verdict, no higher court ever reverses its final word.

Hard and adverse was the life of Jasper! For years many hostile forces sought to unhorse and cripple him. It would require books to hold the slanders and scandals laid to his charge. The archers used poisoned arrows, and often tore his flesh and fancied that they had him, but his bow abode in strength. Meanwhile, the public, that jury of the many, sat still and watched, weighing the evidence, listening to the prosecutors, unravelling conflicting testimony, and feeling the way to justice. In the midst of it all, the brave old chieftain died, while the trial was yet going on. The jury was long silent, but it has spoken at last, and the verdict is, that the name of this veteran of the cross shall be enrolled among the fearless, the faithful, and the immortal. He endured as seeing the invisible and now he sees.

XIII
THE SUN DO MOVE

IN presenting John Jasper's celebrated sermon on "De Sun Do Move, "I beg to introduce it with several explanatory words. As intimated in a former chapter it is of a dual character. It includes an extended discussion, after his peculiar fashion, of the text, "The Lord God is a man of war; the Lord is His name." Much that he said in that part of his sermon is omitted, only so much being retained as indicates his view of the rotation of the sun. It was really when he came into this part of his sermon that he showed to such great advantage, even though so manifestly in error as to the position which he tried so manfully to antagonize. It was of that combative type of public speech which always put him before the people at his best. I never heard this sermon but once, but I have been amply aided in reproducing it by an elaborate and altogether friendly report of the sermon published at the time by *The Richmond Dispatch*. Jasper opened his discourse with a tender reminiscence and quite an ingenious exordium.

"Low me ter say," he spoke with an outward composure which revealed an inward but mastered swell of emotion, "dat when I wuz a young man and a slave, I knowed nuthin' wuth talkin' 'bout consarnin' books. Dey wuz sealed mysteries ter me, but I tell yer I longed ter break de seal. I thusted fer de bread uv learnin'. When I seen books I ached ter git in ter um, fur I knowed dat dey had de stuff fer me, an' I wanted ter taste dere contents, but most of de time dey wuz bar'd aginst me.

"By de mursy of de Lord a thing happened. I got er room-feller--he wuz a slave, too, an' he had learn'd ter read. In de dead uv de night he giv me lessons outen de New York Spellin' book. It wuz hard pullin', I tell yer; harder on him, fur he know'd jes' a leetle, an' it made him sweat ter try ter beat sumthin' inter my hard haid. It wuz wuss wid me. Up de hill ev'ry step, but when I got de light uv de less'n into my noodle I farly shouted, but I kno'd I wuz not a scholur. De consequens wuz I crep 'long mighty tejus, gittin' a crum here an' dar untel I cud read de Bible by skippin' de long words, tolerable well. Dat wuz de start uv my eddicashun--dat is, wat little I got. I mek menshun uv dat young man. De years hev fled erway sense den, but I ain't furgot my teachur, an' nevur shall. I thank mer Lord fur him, an' I carries his mem'ry in my heart.

" 'Bout seben months after my gittin' ter readin', Gord cunverted my soul, an' I reckin 'bout de fust an' main thing dat I begged de Lord ter give me wuz de power ter und'stan' His Word. I ain' braggin', an' I hates self-praise, but I boun' ter speak de thankful word. I b'lieves in mer heart dat mer pra'r ter und'stand de Scripshur wuz heard. Sence dat time I ain't keerd 'bout nuthin' 'cept ter study an' preach de Word uv God.

"Not, my bruthrin, dat I'z de fool ter think I knows it all. Oh, mer Father, no! Fur frum it. I don' hardly und'stan myse'f, nor ha'f uv de things roun' me, an' dar is milyuns uv things in de Bible too deep fur Jasper, an' sum uv 'em too deep fur ev'rybody. I doan't cerry de' keys ter de Lord's closet, an' He ain' tell me ter peep in, an' ef I did I'm so stupid I wouldn't know it when I see it. No, frens, I knows my place at de feet uv my Marster, an' dar I stays.

"But I kin read de Bible and git de things whar lay on de top uv de soil. Out'n de Bible I knows nuthin' extry 'bout de sun. I sees 'is courses as he rides up dar so gran' an' mighty in de sky, but dar is heaps 'bout dat flamin' orb dat is too much fer me. I know dat de sun shines powerfly an' po's down its light in floods, an' yet dat is nuthin' compared wid de light dat flashes in my min' frum de pages of Gord's book. But you knows all dat. I knows dat de sun burns--oh, how it did burn in dem July days. I tell yer he cooked de skin on my back many er day when I wuz hoein' in de corn feil'. But you knows all dat, an' yet dat is nuthin' der to de divine fire dat burns in der souls uv Gord's chil'n. Can't yer feel it, bruthrin?

"But 'bout de courses uv de sun, I have got dat. I hev dun rang'd thru de whole blessed book an' scode down de las' thing de Bible has ter say 'bout de' movements uv de sun. I got all dat pat an' safe. An' lemme say dat if I doan't giv it ter you straight, if I gits one word crooked or wrong, you jes' holler out, 'Hol' on dar, Jasper, yer ain't got dat straight,' an' I'll beg pardon. If I doan't tell de truf, march up on dese steps here an' tell me I'z a liar, an' I'll take it. I fears I do lie sometimes--I'm so sinful, I find it hard ter do right; but my Gord doan't lie an' He ain' put no lie in de Book uv eternal truf, an' if I giv you wat de Bible say, den I boun' ter tell de truf.

"I got ter take yer all dis arternoon on er skershun ter a great bat'l feil'. Mos' folks like ter see fights--some is mighty fon' er gittin' inter fights, an' some is mighty quick ter run down de back alley when dar is a bat'l goin' on, fer de right. Dis time I'll 'scort yer ter a scene whar you shall witness a curus bat'l. It tuk place soon arter Isrel got in de Promus Lan'. Yer 'member de people uv Gibyun mak frens wid Gord's people when dey fust entered Canum an' dey wuz monsus smart ter do it. But, jes' de same, it got 'em in ter an orful fuss. De cities roun' 'bout dar flar'd up at dat, an' dey all jined dere forces and say dey gwine ter mop de Gibyun people orf uv de groun', an' dey bunched all dar armies tergedder an' went up fer ter do it. Wen dey kum up so bol' an' brave de Giby'nites wuz skeer'd out'n dere senses, an' dey saunt word ter Joshwer dat dey wuz in troubl' an' he mus' run up dar an' git 'em out. Joshwer had de heart uv a lion an' he wuz up dar d'reckly. Dey had an orful fight, sharp an' bitter, but yer might know dat Ginr'l Joshwer wuz not up dar ter git whip't. He prayed an' he fought, an' de hours got erway too peart fer him, an' so he ask'd de Lord ter issure a speshul ordur dat de sun hol' up erwhile an' dat de moon furnish plenty uv moonshine down on de lowes' part uv de fightin' groun's. As a fac', Joshwer wuz so drunk wid de bat'l, so thursty fer de blood uv de en'mies uv de Lord, an' so wild wid de vict'ry dat he tell de sun ter stan' still tel he cud finish his job. Wat did de sun do? Did he glar down in fi'ry wrath an' say, 'What you talkin' 'bout my stoppin' for, Joshwer; I ain't navur startid yit. Bin here all de time, an' it wud smash up ev'rything if I wuz ter start'? Naw, he ain' say dat. But wat de Bible say? Dat's wat I ax ter know. It say dat it wuz at de voice uv Joshwer dat it stopped. I don' say it stopt; tain't fer Jasper ter say dat, but de Bible, de Book uv Gord, say so. But I say dis; nuthin' kin stop untel it hez fust startid. So I knows wat I'm talkin' 'bout. De sun wuz travlin' long dar thru de sky wen de order come. He hitched his red ponies and made quite a call on de lan' uv Gibyun. He purch up dar in de skies jes' as frenly as a naibur whar comes ter borrer sumthin', an' he stan' up dar an' he look lak he enjoyed de way Joshwer waxes dem wicked armies. An' de moon, she wait down in de low groun's dar, an' pours out her light and look jes' as ca'm an' happy as if she wuz waitin' fer her 'scort. Dey nevur budg'd, neither uv 'em, long as de Lord's army needed er light to kerry on de bat'l.

"I doan't read when it wuz dat Joshwer hitch up an' drove on, but I 'spose it wuz when de Lord toll him ter go. Ennybody knows dat de sun didn' stay dar all de time. It stopt fur bizniz, an' went on when it got thru. Dis is 'bout all dat I has ter do wid dis perticl'r case. I dun show'd yer dat dis part uv de Lord's word teaches yer dat de sun stopt, which show dat he wuz movin' befo' dat, an' dat he went on art'rwuds. I toll yer dat I wud prove dis an' I's dun it, an' I derfies ennybody to say dat my p'int ain't made.

"I tol' yer in de fust part uv dis discose dat de Lord Gord is a man uv war. I 'spec by now yer begin ter see it is so. Doan't yer admit it?

When de Lord cum ter see Joshwer in de day uv his feers an' warfar, an' actu'ly mek de sun stop stone still in de heavuns, so de fight kin rage on tel all de foes is slain, yer bleeged ter und'rstan' dat de Gord uv peace is also de man uv war. He kin use bofe peace an' war ter hep de reichus, an' ter scattur de host uv de ailyuns. A man talked ter me las' week 'bout de laws uv nature, an' he say dey carn't poss'bly be upsot, an' I had ter laugh right in his face. As if de laws uv ennythin' wuz greater dan my Gord who is de lawgiver fer ev'rything. My Lord is great; He rules in de heavuns, in de earth, an' doun und'r de groun'. He is great, an' greatly ter be praised. Let all de people bow doun an' wurship befo' Him!

"But let us git erlong, for dar is quite a big lot mo' comin' on. Let us take nex' de case of Hezekier. He wuz one of dem kings of Juder--er mighty sorry lot I mus' say dem kings wuz, fur de mos' part. I inclines ter think Hezekier wuz 'bout de highes' in de gin'ral avrig, an' he war no mighty man hisse'f. Well, Hezekier he got sick. I dar say dat a king when he gits his crown an' fin'ry off, an' when he is posterated wid mortal sickness, he gits 'bout es commun lookin' an' grunts an' rolls, an' is 'bout es skeery as de res' of us po' mortals. We know dat Hezekier wuz in er low state uv min'; full uv fears, an' in a tur'ble trub'le. De fac' is, de Lord strip him uv all his glory an' landed him in de dust. He tol' him dat his hour had come, an' dat he had bettur squar up his affaars, fur death wuz at de do'. Den it wuz dat de king fell low befo' Gord; he turn his face ter de wall; he cry, he moan, he beg'd de Lord not ter take him out'n de worl' yit. Oh, how good is our Gord! De cry uv de king moved his heart, an' he tell him he gwine ter give him anudder show. Tain't only de kings dat de Lord hears. De cry uv de pris'nur, de wail uv de bondsman, de tears uv de dyin' robber, de prars uv de backslider, de sobs uv de womun dat wuz a sinner, mighty apt to tech de heart uv de Lord. It look lik it's hard fer de sinner ter git so fur orf or so fur down in de pit dat his cry can't reach de yere uv de mussiful Saviour.

"But de Lord do evun better den dis fur Hezekier-- He tell him He gwine ter give him a sign by which he'd know dat what He sed wuz cummin' ter pars. I ain't erquainted wid dem sun diuls dat de Lord toll Hezekier 'bout, but ennybody dat hes got a grain uv sense knows dat dey wuz de clocks uv dem ole times an' dey marked de travuls uv de sun by dem diuls. When, darfo' Gord tol' de king dat He wud mek de shadder go backwud, it mus' hev bin jes' lak puttin' de han's uv de clock back, but, mark yer, Izaer 'spressly say dat de sun return'd ten dergrees. Thar yer are! Ain't dat de movement uv de sun? Bless my soul. Hezekier's case beat Joshwer. Joshwer stop de sun, but heer de Lord mek de sun walk back ten dergrees; an' yet dey say dat de sun stan' stone still an' nevur move er peg. It look ter me he move roun' mighty brisk an' is ready ter go ennyway dat de Lord ordurs him ter go. I wonder if enny uv dem furloserfers is roun' here dis arternoon. I'd lik ter take a squar' look at one uv dem an' ax him to 'splain dis mattur. He carn't do it, my bruthr'n. He knows a heap 'bout books, maps, figgers an' long distunces, but I derfy him ter take up Hezekier's case an' 'splain it orf. He carn't do' it. De Word uv de Lord is my defense an' bulwurk, an' I fears not what men can say nor do; my Gord gives me de vict'ry.

" 'Low me, my frens, ter put mysef squar 'bout dis movement uv de sun. It ain't no bizniss uv mine wedder de sun move or stan' still, or wedder it stop or go back or rise or set. All dat is out er my han's 'tirely, an' I got nuthin' ter say. I got no the-o-ry on de subjik. All I ax is dat we will take wat de Lord say 'bout it an' let His will be dun 'bout ev'rything. Wat dat will is I karn't know 'cept He whisper inter my soul or write it in a book. Here's de Book. Dis is 'nough fer me, and wid it ter pilut me, I karn't git fur erstray.

"But I ain't dun wid yer yit. As de song says, dere's mo' ter foller. I envite yer ter heer

de fust vers in de sev'nth chaptur uv de book uv Reverlashuns. What do John, und'r de pow'r uv de Spirit, say? He say he saw fo' anguls standin' on de fo' corners uv de earth, holdin' de fo' win's uv de earth, an' so fo'th.

'Low me ter ax ef de earth is roun', whar do it keep its corners? Er flat, squar thing has corners, but tell me where is de cornur uv er appul, ur a marbul, ur a cannun ball, ur a silver dollar. Ef dar is enny one uv dem furloserfurs whar's been takin' so many cracks at my ole haid 'bout here, he is korjully envited ter step for'd an' squar up dis vexin' bizniss. I here tell you dat yer karn't squar a circul, but it looks lak dese great scolurs dun learn how ter circul de squar. Ef dey kin do it, let 'em step ter de front an' do de trick. But, mer brutherin, in my po' judmint, dey karn't do it; tain't in 'em ter do it. Dey is on der wrong side of de Bible; dat's on de outside of de Bible, an' dar's whar de trubbul comes in wid 'em. Dey dun got out uv de bres'wuks uv de truf, an' ez long ez dey stay dar de light uv de Lord will not shine on der path. I ain't keer'n so much 'bout de sun, tho' it's mighty kunveenyunt ter hav it, but my trus' is in de Word uv de Lord. Long ez my feet is flat on de solid rock, no man kin move me. I'se gittin' my order fum de Gord of my salvashun.

"Tother day er man wid er hi coler and side whisk'rs cum ter my house. He was one nice North'rn gemman wat think a heap of us col'rd people in de Souf. Da ar luvly folks and I honours 'em very much. He seem from de start kinder strictly an' cross wid me, and arter while, he brake out furi'us and frettid, an' he say: 'Erlow me Mister Jasper ter gib you sum plain advise. Dis nonsans 'bout de sun movin' whar you ar gettin' is disgracin' yer race all ober de kuntry, an' as a fren of yer peopul, I cum ter say it's got ter stop.' Ha! Ha! Ha! Mars' Sam Hargrove nuvur hardly smash me dat way. It was equl to one ov dem ole overseurs way bac yondur. I tel him dat ef he'll sho me I'se wrong, I giv it all up.

"My! My! Ha! Ha! He sail in on me an' such er storm about science, nu 'scuv'ries, an' de Lord only knos wat all, I ner hur befo', an' den he tel me my race is ergin me an' po ole Jasper mus shet up 'is fule mouf.

"Wen he got thru--it look lak he nuvur wud, I tel him John Jasper ain' set up to be no scholur, an' doant kno de ferlosophiz, an' ain' tryin' ter hurt his peopul, but is wurkin' day an' night ter lif 'em up, but his foot is on de rock uv eternal truff. Dar he stan' and dar he is goin' ter stan' til Gabrul soun's de judgment note. So er say to de gemman wat scol'd me up so dat I hur him mek his remarks, but I ain' hur whar he get his Scriptu' from, an' dat 'tween him an' de wurd of de Lord I tek my stan' by de Word of Gord ebery time. Jasper ain' mad: he ain' fightin' nobody; he ain' bin 'pinted janitur to run de sun: he nothin' but de servunt of Gord and a luver of de Everlasting Word. What I keer about de sun? De day comes on wen de sun will be called frum his race-trac, and his light squincked out foruvur; de moon shall turn ter blood, and this yearth be konsoomed wid fier. Let um go; dat wont skeer me nor trubble Gord's erlect'd peopul, for de word uv de Lord shell aindu furivur, an' on dat Solid Rock we stan' an' shall not be muved.

"Is I got yer satisfied yit? Has I prooven my p'int? Oh, ye whose hearts is full uv unberlief! Is yer still hol'in' out? I reckun de reason yer say de sun don' move is 'cause yer are so hard ter move yerse'f. You is a reel triul ter me, but, nevur min'; I ain't gi'n yer up yit, an' nevur will. Truf is mighty; it kin break de heart uv stone, an' I mus' fire anudder arrur uv truf out'n de quivur uv de Lord. If yer haz er copy uv God's Word 'bout yer pussun, please tu'n ter dat miner profit, Malerki, wat writ der las' book in der ole Bible, an' look at chaptur de fust, vurs 'leben; what do it say? I bet'r read it, fur I got er noshun yer critics doan't kerry enny Bible in thar pockits ev'ry day in de week. Here is wat it says: 'Fur from de risin' uv de sun evun unter de goin' doun uv de same My name shall be great 'mong de Gentiles. . . My name shall be great 'mong de heathun, sez de Lord uv hosts.' How do dat suit yer? It look lak dat ort ter fix it. Dis time it is de Lord uv hosts Hisse'f dat is doin' de talkin', an' He is talkin' on er wonderful an' glorious subjik. He is tellin' uv de spredin' uv His Gorspel, uv de kummin' uv His larst vict'ry ovur de Gentiles, an' de wurldwide glories dat at de las' He is ter git. Oh, my bruddrin, wat er time dat will be. My soul teks wing es I erticipate wid joy dat merlenium day! De glories as dey shine befo' my eyes blin's me, an' I furgits de sun an' moon an' stars. I jes' 'members dat 'long 'bout dose las' days dat de sun an moon will go out uv bizniss, fur dey won' be needed no mo'. Den will King Jesus come back ter see His people, an' He will be de suffishunt light uv de wurl'. Joshwer's bat'ls will be ovur. Hezekier woan't

JOHN JASPER

need no sun diul, an' de sun an' moon will fade out befo'
de glorius splendurs uv de New Jerruslem.

"But wat der mattur wid Jasper. I mos' furgit my
bizniss, an' mos' gon' ter shoutin' ovur de far away glories
uv de secun' cummin' uv my Lord. I beg pardun, an' will
try ter git back ter my subjik. I hev ter do as de sun in
Hezekier's case--fall back er few dergrees. In dat part uv
de Word dat I gin yer frum Malerki--dat de Lord Hisse'f
spoke--He klars dat His glory is gwine ter spred. Spred?
Whar? Frum de risin' uv de sun ter de goin' down uv de
same. Wat? Doan't say dat, duz it? Dat's edzakly wat it
sez. Ain't dat cleer 'nuff fer yer? De Lord pity dese
doubtin' Tommusses. Here is 'nuff ter settul it all an' kure
de wuss cases. Walk up yere, wise folks, an' git yer
med'sin. Whar is dem high collar'd furloserfurs now? Wat
dey skulkin' roun' in de brush fer? Why doan't yer git out
in der broad arternoon light an' fight fer yer cullurs? Ah, I
un'stans it; yer got no answer. De Bible is agin yer, an' in
yer konshunses yer are convictid.

"But I hears yer back dar. Wat yer wisprin' 'bout? I
know; yer say yer sont me sum papurs an' I nevur answer
dem. Ha, ha, ha! I got 'em. De differkulty 'bout dem
papurs yer sont me is dat dey did not answer me. Dey
nevur menshun de Bible one time. Yer think so much uv
yoursef's an' so little uv de Lord Gord an' thinks wat yer
say is so smart dat yer karn't even speak uv de Word uv
de Lord. When yer ax me ter stop believin' in de Lord's
Word an' ter pin my faith ter yo words, I ain't er gwine ter

142

do it. I take my stan' by de Bible an' res' my case on wat it says. I take wat de Lord says 'bout my sins, 'bout my Saviour, 'bout life, 'bout death, 'bout de wurl' ter come, an' I take wat de Lord say 'bout de sun an' moon, an' I cares little wat de haters of mer Gord chooses ter say. Think dat I will fursake de Bible? It is my only Book, my hope, de arsnel uv my soul's surplies, an' I wants nuthin' else.

"But I got ernudder wurd fur yer yit. I done wuk ovur dem. papurs dat yer sont me widout date an' widout yer name. Yer deals in figgurs an' thinks yer are biggur dan de arkanjuls. Lemme see wat yer dun say. Yer set yerse'f up ter tell me how fur it is frum here ter de sun. Yer think yer got it down ter er nice p'int. Yer say it is 3,339,002 miles frum de earth ter de sun. Dat's wat yer say. Nudder one say dat de distuns is 12,000,000; nudder got it ter 27,000,000. I hers dat de great Isuk Nutun wuk't it up ter 28,000,000, an' later on de furloserfurs gin ernudder rippin' raze to 50,000,000. De las' one gits it bigger' dan all de yuthers, up to 90,000,000. Doan't enny uv 'em ergree edzakly an' so dey runs a guess game, an' de las' guess is always de bigges'. Now, wen dese guessers kin hav a kunvenshun in Richmun' an' all ergree 'pun de same thing, I'd be glad ter hear frum yer ag'in, an' I duz hope dat by dat time yer won't be ershamed uv yer name.

"Heeps uv railroads hes bin built sense I saw de fust one wen I wuz fifteen yeers ole, but I ain't hear tell uv er railroad built yit ter de sun. I doan' see why ef dey kin meshur de distuns ter de sun, dey might not git up er railroad er a telurgraf an' enabul us ter fin' sumthin' else 'bout it den merely how fur orf de sun is. Dey tell me dat a kannun ball cu'd mek de trep ter de sun in twelve years. Why doan' dey send it? It might be rig'd up wid quarturs fur a few furloserfers on de inside an' fixed up fur er kumfurterble ride. Dey wud need twelve years' rashuns an' a heep uv changes uv ramint--mighty thick clo'es wen dey start and mighty thin uns wen dey git dar.

"Oh, mer bruthrin, dese things mek yer laugh, an' I doan' blem yer fer laughin', 'cept it's always sad ter laugh at der follies uv fools. If we cu'd laugh 'em out'n kount'nens, we might well laugh day an' night. Wat cuts inter my soul is, dat all dese men seem ter me dat dey is hittin' at de Bible. Dat's wat sturs my soul an' fills me wid reichus wrath. Leetle keers I wat dey says 'bout de sun, purvided dey let de Word uv de Lord erlone. But nevur min'. Let de heethun rage an' de people 'madgin er vain thing. Our King shall break 'em in pieces an' dash 'em down. But blessed be de name uv our Gord, de Word uv de Lord indurith furivur. Stars may fall, moons may turn ter blood, an' de sun set ter rise no mo', but Thy kingdom, oh, Lord, is frum evurlastin' ter evurlastin'.

"But I has er word dis arternoon fer my own brutherin. Dey is de people fer whose souls I got ter watch--fur dem I got ter stan' an' report at de last--dey is my sheep an' I'se der shepherd, an' my soul is knit ter dem forever. 'Tain fer me ter be troublin' yer wid dese questions erbout dem heb'nly bodies. Our eyes goes far beyon' de smaller stars; our home is clean outer sight uv dem twinklin' orbs; de chariot dat will cum ter take us to our Father's mansion will sweep out by dem flickerin' lights an' never halt till it brings us in clar view uv de throne uv de Lamb. Doan't hitch yer hopes to no sun nor stars; yer home is got Jesus fer its light, an' yer hopes mus' trabel up dat way. I preach dis sermon jest fer ter settle de min's uv my few brutherin, an' repeats it 'cause kin' frens wish ter hear it, an' I hopes it will do honour ter de Lord's Word. But nuthin' short of de purly gates can satisfy me, an' I charge, my people, fix yer feet on de solid Rock, yer hearts on Calv'ry, an' yer eyes on de throne uv de Lamb. Dese strifes an' griefs 'll soon git ober; we shall see de King in His glory an' be at ease. Go on, go on, ye ransom uv de Lord; shout His praises as yer go, an' I shall meet yer in de city uv de New Jeruserlum, whar we shan't need the light uv de sun, fer de Lam' uv de Lord is de light uv de saints."

XIV
ONE JASPER DAY IN THE SPRING TIME OF 1878
The Story of a Spectator

THE paper which follows is a composite, embodying many incidents and facts connected with the Jasper sensation, and designed to reflect, so far as possible, the impression made by the fiery old philosopher upon those who though out of sympathy with his astronomical notions fell as helpless victims beneath the spell of his eloquence and honesty.

For quite a while the Jasper sensation had grown acute in Richmond. Beginning as a freak, it bloomed into a fad, got in the air, and actually invaded private homes. It was a pentecost for the curious, a juicy apple for the hard-driven reporter, a festival for the scoffer, and a roaring financial bonanza for the saints of Sixth Mount Zion.

I confess that, for my part, it struck me as a ridiculous business at best, the big bubble of an hour, and that if not caught at the exact moment it would speedily disappear, and while I was a sprig of a reporter it was the sort of thing which did not come my way. Being, however, of a prying and curious turn of mind I determined to take one glimpse at the black elephant. It took time, however, to get my purpose into working order, but my day came in due course. I awoke one morning to find the Saturday papers "festering" with Jasper. He was in the advertisements, in the communications, and in the local columns, and the show was to come off the next day. They told once more of his astronomical absurdities, as I believed them to be, and informed me that the exhibition would come off at 3 P. M. on the next afternoon. At noon, I dropped into Reugers' for my lunch, and a table of hayseed legislators were filling the room, with noisy gabble about Jasper and his planetary crochets. I found that some of them had signed a paper asking for the approaching Jasperian exhibition, and others of them were twitting and punching them for their folly; but I found that both sides of them were going.

Later in the day, I got into a West Main Street car and found a seat next to three ladies who evidently had a serious attack of Jasper, and they, too, were bargaining to go. At the supper table in my boarding-house that evening I found a sickly old Yankee minister loafing in Richmond for his health, in a swivet of excitement about Jasper and his coming oration. My landlady's fourteen year old boy told me that his mother had promised that he should go to hear Jasper, on the hampering condition that he could get some

gentleman to go with him, and his appeal for my company would have beaten Jasper in the point of passionate eloquence. To me, it all seemed a stew of folly, and yet I found myself gratified to have this earnest lad as an excuse in favour of my going.

I finally bargained with the eager youngster that I would waylay him the next morning on his early escape from the Sunday-school, and we would stroll out into the vicinity of the Sixth Mount Zion Church, and make a preliminary reconnoissance of the general situation. We did not find it quite a well-odoured stroll at all points, particularly as we got in the neighbourhood of the church, for we encountered a tangle of streets and alleys some of which were not in the best condition.

Not long after crossing Broad Street we began to run afoul of squads and groups of coloured people, and the total strain of their chat was Jasper and what was coming later on. The nearer we came to the church, the combat, as the poet said, deepened, that is, the groups multiplied and the Jasperian element grew. A huge negro woman hanging on a side-gate on Clay Street was shouting in a piping voice about Jasper and the sun, and telling to several dumb listeners that "she wuz gwine ter be dar ef de Lord 'sparred' her an' it wuz de las' thing she done on de yerth."

I observed also several of those Virginia solons already mentioned,--those big footed, badly shaven, and consequential legislators,--prowling in the neighbourhood of the church, as if they were studying and planning for burglaries. As we meandered the crooked streets which admitted us to a sight of the great Sixth Mount Zion, we saw in every direction the sign of a prodigious expectancy. Front yards, streets, and alleys had their contingents, and you could not get within ear-shot without getting some novel and surprising hints as to John Jasper and the Solar System. We could hear singing in the church, and we assumed that something in the way of worship was in process. That, however, was not IT. That was a tame and pithless performance, and if Jasper was in it at all he was evidently resting his better forces for the bigger battle at three o'clock in the impending afternoon.

The attraction on the inside was out of gear and didn't draw. My young companion, who was vastly my superior as to the Jasper situation, informed me with marked conviction that the thing for us to do, and to do at once and with a rush, was to go back to the house, swallow our dinner, and get back with the utmost speed. We did not get away, however, before we noted that all avenues in the vicinity of the church seemed to be filling. Some were coming and going; some were knotted into groups looking very solemn and apparently awestruck, and some were crowding in like late comers at a circus; but whenever you caught a word it had to do with Jasper. As we walked away, the son of my landlady, full of the fidgets and outraged by my slow motion remarked sagely: "Ain't he got 'em?" I had to admit it; he had 'em,--by a grip tighter than if he had 'em by the nape of the neck. Evidently enough, he had them, and in a bunch as big as the town.

But I didn't know it fully then. Being untutored in Jasper's holding power, I was fresh enough to suppose that all that buzzing, swarming gang of negroes would scatter away to their frugal Sunday meal, and that the alleys and streets would empty into their usual vacancy, though the boy's mien of hurry and eagerness was warning me to the contrary. He mentioned several times that from what other boys had told him we must go very early, and in order to gratify him we got out of the boarding-house at a quarter after one, and we needed only fifteen minutes of quiet walking to get a front seat.

Shades of the Pharaohs and shadows of the Pyramids! As we headed towards the seat of planetary conflict the streets looked like black rivers. Great lines of blacks, relieved here and there by companies of whites, thronged the sidewalks. Were Hannibal's Carthagenian legions being turned loose in Richmond? Or had some mighty earthquake ripped open the foundations of Richmond, and were the people, caked with the soot, fleeing for life? It was more tranquil than that, thank heaven! It was however the town, upheaved and agitated, striving fiercely for Sixth Mount Zion, to hear the supreme sensation of all his race,--as I now began to realize he was. Squares before we got to the church we collided with the returning tide. "No use of going," they said,--"house already packed; streets full, men fighting and women fainting," and a deal more of the-same sort.

But these appalling things only urged me on. If there was to be a congestion or a catastrophe, it was just to my taste as well as to my profession to attend. Besides, I had in me a desperate purpose to get into that house, and I promised the boy that we'd sink or swim together. I understood it was perfectly scriptural to rip off the roof as the last resort. The occasion had jumped the common road, and it was folly to falter now before any obstacle. The fight through that mob has left me some marks to be noticed when I am dressed for my burial. My toes were tramped into jelly. At one time I was lifted by a rush, and one of my knees aches yet in bad weather as a consequence. Several times I thought the landlady's boy was doomed to become an unrecognizable mangle. It began to sift into me that Jasper was more than a man, and nothing short of an entire situation and a public menace. My business was more and more to see him.

The church, when first seen, looked like a tall boat borne on the heads of thousands, and yet I pushed along. Now, right here, I have to drop my honesty and become a hypocrite. How I got into that house must not be told. There is a muscular, ginger-bread fellow who stays in the office down town, and he broke all rules and I know not how many bones, and, miraculous as it was, landed me and the boy into the pulpit with blood on the boy's nose.

Now, excuse me from describing the music and the praying, though I would like to mention that the song that the old darkey in the Amen corner with the white nape and the quivering voice started up, and which it looked to me like all the people in the world were singing, rather jerked me out of myself and took me off on its waves, and when I got back I had to use my handkerchief in an unusual way.

Jasper made a prayer also, and the way he talked to the Lord about his own meanness and his ignorance, knocked out of me about half of my notion that he was a dribbling old egotist and numbskull. He caused cold chills to pass up my back by several surprising things which he said to the Lord in a most serious way, and I have to own that by the time he said "Amen," I was a little prejudiced in his favour.

Further, allow me to say right here that I know positively that I never saw so many people in a house of that size at one time as was in the church that afternoon. Women sat in each other's laps, the pulpit was piled up, and all the spaces chinked, packed, and doubled up. I ought to add that the look of eagerness, expectation, and attention was oppressive. No whispering, no looking around; only silence, except when Jasper started them. Then you felt the mastery and the subduing sovereignty of the man. I saw that the white people had been favoured in getting seats, and there were hordes of them. The legislators abounded, and there were preachers, lawyers, notable men, fashionable women, and not a few strangers in Richmond, all herding together and very serious. It wasn't, I confess, what I expected. I looked for a circus, and had hooked a funeral,--no, not a funeral; it wasn't dismal enough for that, but far more thoughtful and wakeful than a funeral can be.

I looked Jasper over with a critical eye, and before he began to preach I had his age down for sixty-two, but when he began to career over the pulpit I knocked off ten years. He had an unattractive bulge on his face around his cheekbone, but his head looked like an alpine cliff. His eye, I noted, was an all sufficient redeemer, and its flash and laugh would cover acres of ugliness. His whiskers were decidedly undistinguished, except in their cut, and I marked his blood as unmixed. He dressed in a manner best suited to prevent people from noticing how he dressed, and his tall form and alert action made him attractive in the pulpit.

During the sermon he had something to say about himself. "I'll be sixty-six years old on de fo'th day uv dis coming July. I set out ter seek de salvation uv my Gord in 1839. I have never been in any school, but I spent some months trying ter learn ter spell. I wuz converted in Marse Sam Hargrove's terbakur fac'try in dis city, on de 25th day uv July, 1839, and frum dat day I have know'd dat Gord had anintid me wid de Holy Ghost ter preach de Gorspil uv His Son."

You couln't hear Jasper say that and doubt. He seemed to assert a mastery over me from the start as to his sincerity. It was impossible, moreover, to question the honesty of anything he said. He made another remark at the outset which made everybody smile, but it was not a frivolous smile by a long shot. He said he was so ignorant when he first felt he must preach that he thought maybe God wouldn't want a man to preach who could not read, and that maybe the devil had put that notion into him. Then he stopped, and with a decided smile he said, "I got a notion dat ef de debbul put dis thing in me, den he wuz a bigger fool dan I ever thought he cud be. I don't think he hav made much by settin' me out ter preach ef he did fer I done knocked his kingdom hard blows many a day, but arter more dan forty years servin' my Gord I know who I hev b'lieved. I feel dat wenever I stan' up in His name, de Lord is wid me."

After these remarks he gave out his text and started in.

"Ef I don't prove ter you by de word uv my Gord ter day dat de sun do move, den I ergree never ter preach agin es long es my head is 'bove de clods. I spek ebbry lady an' gentl'man presunt dis evenin' ter say wedder wat I say is so or not, arter dey hear wat I hav ter say. I'll speak out'n de Bibul, an' I want evrybody ter mark de words dat I giv 'em."

I found that Jasper had a keen eye for business. He did things according to the book. He had ferreted out of the Bible every passage that bore upon the motions of the sun, and he had them all printed in a sort of tract. A copy of these passages he placed in the hands of every one who could read and wished to follow him. He stumbled considerably over the big words, but he skipped none, and kept along, and when he would read a passage he would ask to be corrected if, in any small degree, he had not read it as it ought to be. He was greatly set on doing clean work, and not seeming to be willing to fool anybody

After reading a passage, then "the fun" would begin. He would pluck out of it the part that helped his argument, and it was a sight to see him with this passage as if it were a broad sword. He would charge upon his antagonists, shouting and laughing, and whacking them as he went until he would close that part of his work in a storm of eloquence. How he did move the people! He moved with the stride of the conqueror.

I am not skilled in religious reporting and cannot undertake to follow Jasper in that fusillade of comment and criticism with which, for a full hour and a half, he bore down upon his adversaries, crashing and scattering them as he went. A few of his sayings, however, stuck. He drove them into my flesh like fangs, and possibly a concrete show of them may help outsiders towards a conclusion as to what Jasper is after.

His text, so far as I could see, was not within ninety-five millions of miles of the question as to the movement of the sun. It did however suit exactly for that part of his sermon which had to do with the Lord as the defender of

155

His ancient people. He grew vivid in picturing ancient Israel travelling through the great wilderness, and in showing how God delivered them from all their foes.

His wonder as an orator broke out in unmeasured splendour as he portrayed the power of God at the crossing of the Red Sea. A pathetic spectacle were the Hebrew slaves, as they fled out of Egypt pursued by the embattled legions of Pharaoh. As the Lord's people, as he called them, got hemmed up with the sea in front of them and the great armies charging in the rear, he actually made the people cry in dread and terror lest these refugees should be totally extinguished. The scene was so lifelike and overmastering that shudders swept through the crowd, and women were wild with actual fright. Then when Moses came; when the rod was stretched over the sea and the waters, as if appalled by the presence of the Lord God, began to part and roll back until they left a clear passage between;--why everybody could see it. It was as plain as a great road in the broad daylight, and as the Hebrews, with revived hope, in solid columns, moved across, his people took fire; they literally shouted the children of Israel over. Jasper himself was leading the host, cheering, shouting to them not to be afraid, and telling them that God would bring them safely through. It looked to me as if half of the women were clapping their hands or dancing, and the other half were rolling off the benches in the excess of their rapture, as the last of the children of Israel came trudging out upon the banks.

But instantaneously Jasper brought a revulsion of feeling. He discovered the vast host of Pharaoh marching with music and with banners through the parted walls of the Red Sea. *They* were coming too! After all, the people had shouted too soon. The triumphant Egyptians would soon be upon them, and the chosen of the Lord, after all, must be destroyed.

Why, look! The host is half-across; three-fourths now, getting nearer and nearer. "Oh, my God," Jasper cried, with a shriek of despair. "Help! Help! or Thy people will be blotted out."

All over the house there were sobs and groans and cries of fright. Once more the hand of the master was upon them, and he swayed them as he would. Then with a shout he cried: "De walls of de Red Sea are fallin'! De partid waturs rush inter each udder's imbrace. Oh, ye heavens, shout an' let de earth be glad. Let hell ter its mos' remotes' dep's quake and cry: 'De Lord Gord is a man uv war. De Lord is His name!' Tell de tidin's. Shout it everywhar dat Gord hav' delivured His people."

I have always liked fine speaking. Oratory has a resistless charm for me. I bow to the man who thrills me. If Jasper wasn't the soul of eloquence that day, then I know not what eloquence is. He painted scene after scene. He lifted the people to the sun and sank them down to despair. He plucked them out of hard places and filled them with shouting. As long as I live all that Red Sea business, with Egypt and the fleeing Hebrews and Pharaoh and his great legions and the sea and the ruin and the great deliverance, are mine to keep as long as my mental powers can act. True, Jasper made me ridiculous three or four times by so convulsing me with laughter that I wanted to roll on the floor, but it didn't make me frivolous a bit. I never knew that wit was such a deep and serious thing before.

The old orator had to stop "to blow" awhile, and it was a strictly original noise he made, as he refilled his exhausted lungs with a fresh supply of oxygen. The rush of air fairly shook the glass in the windows and could have been heard perhaps for a square off. All at once his face began to brighten with a smile, which almost amounted to an illumination. He said it "kinder 'mused him ter ubsurv Gord's keen way uv wurryin' Pharo' inter lettin' His people go."

I am a failure on dialect, but this part of the afternoon's entertainment came with such surprise that it was photographed on my memory in a way it can never be blotted out. Jasper took up the several plagues which he asserted that God sent upon the Egyptian monarch, declaring that as Pharo' was too much of a brute to hear reason, or to feel afraid, the Lord decided to tease and torment him with reptiles and insects, and then he added: "I tell yer, my brudderin, dis skeme did de buzniss fer Pharo'. He kum frum ridin' one day an' wen he git in de pallis de hole hall is full uv frogs. Dey iz scamperrin' and hoppin' roun' tel dey farly kivur de groun' an' Pharo' put his big foot an' squash'd 'em on de marbul flo'. He run inter his parler tryin' ter git away frum 'em. Dey wuz all erroun'; on de fine chars, on de lounges, in de pianner. It shocked de king til' he git sick. Jes' den de dinner bell ring, an' in he go ter git his dinner. Ha, ha, ha! It's frogs, frogs, frogs all erroun'! Wen he sot down he felt de frogs squirmin' in de char; de frogs on de plates, squattin' up on de meat, playin' ovur de bred, an' wen he pick up his glas ter drink de watur de little frogs iz swimmin' in de tum'ler. Wen he tried ter stick up a pickul his fork stuck in a frog; he felt him runnin' down his back. De queen she cried, and mos' faintid an' tol' Pharo' dat she wud quit de pallis befo' sundown ef he didn't do somthin' ter cler dem frogs out'n de house. She say she know wat iz de mattur; twuz de Gord uv dem low-down Hebrews, an' she wantid him ter git 'em out uv de country. Pharo' say he wud, but he wuz an awful liar; jes' es dey tel me dat mos' uv de pollitishuns iz."

Just then my vagrant eye caught the string of legislators who had high seats in the synagogue and it looked to me as if every Senegambian in that seething herd was sampling those rustic statesmen while they took on an awfully silly look; or rather I think it was on most of them before. "I can't pikshur up all dem plagues, but I mus' giv you more 'sperunce uv dem brutish people in de pallis dat wuz so cruel ter de Hebrew folk. One mornin' de king wake up an' he wuz ackin' from hed ter foot. He farly scratch'd his skin off his body, an' out he jumps, an' as I liv' he finds hisse'f farly civured ovur wid vermin. 'Bout dat time de queen, she springs up, an' sich scratchin' an' hollerrin' Pharo' nevur herd frum her befo', an' when he look at her dey is crawlin' all over her an' she, fergitten her queenship, iz dashin' erroun' de room shakin' her rappurs an' scratchin' and screamin' tel presn'tly she brek loose on de king agin. 'Bout dat time dar wuz a yell in de nussery, an' in kums de little Pharoes an' dey runs scratchin' and hollerin' an' kickin' ter der mudder. Der heds wuz full wid 'em; dere hands wuz all bit an' swell'd, an' wen der mudder jerk'd off der nite gowns jes' thousans uv'em iz runnin' over'em frum hed ter foot. Pharo' wuz rich, but riches don't kill fleas. Pharo' had big armis, but soljeers can't conquer an army of lice. Pharo' had servunts by de thousans, but all uv'em put togedder cudn't pertek' dem little Pharoes an' princesses frum dat plague dat an angry Gord sent ter skurge Pharo' an' mek 'im willin' ter let His chil'n go."

This is a sample. Jasper's imagination was like a prairie on fire. The excitement in the congregation was of a new order; he was tickling them in a new spot, or rather in forty spots at once, and the noise in the house was almost like the roar of a tempest. I never was in such a conglomerate mood. His picture of the plagues convulsed me with laughter,--would have killed me dead, I verily believe, but for the counteracting effect of the horror excited in me. And more than that, the trials of the Hebrew slaves loomed up before me all the time. I was subconsciously pitying them, and anxious to get my fingers on the damnable throat of the tyrant. I never knew what it was, until that day, to have all sorts of feelings at the same time. It seemed to me that the strain would have to be ended without going further.

But Jasper wasn't done, and things were coming on which it was impossible to foresee. Suddenly I found Jasper on a new trail. This time it was what he called the assassination of Isaac. I discovered that Jasper could talk quite grammatically when he was on his dignity; but, when he struck the abandon and lawlessness of his imagination, he dropped back into his dialect and then he was at his greatest I found also that he delighted in ponderous and sesquipidalian words. He rolled them under his tongue,--save when the words themselves sometimes rolled his tongue up,--and when he hit assassination, the pronunciation would have made a thoughtful mule smile. But the word was simply a bit of dynamite to blow up his crowd and to kindle new flames in his fancy.

Jasper's picture of Abraham had the flavour of a poem. He stood him up on a lofty pedestal, painted him as a man without a vice;-- the pink of a gentleman, the prince of his tribe, the companion of the Lord God, the faithful father and the Father of the Faithful. Since that day, whenever I get tired or feel that I have done something mean, and want to give my moral nature a set up, I recall Jasper's poem on Abraham.

The incident upon which he fastened was the tragical story of the sacrifice of Isaac. He told how the Lord waked Abraham up at night and tickled the old gentleman with the thought that there were some new honours coming on for Isaac, and then in a flash, commanded him to take the boy and go on a three days' run to a mountain and kill and burn him up. The way he portrayed the mental and emotional conflicts of Abraham during those days was like a steel pointed plow in the soil of the soul. Then when they got in sight of the mountain and Abraham halted the cavalcade, and he and the boy, parting from the rest, set out to climb the mountain alone I got mad and felt like ripping the whole schedule into fragments. There was a deadly hush on the crowd. The air was tense, and all who were capable of it turned pale. Just then Jasper gave a slight jerk to the turn of things and came to my relief.

"Why yer reckin Gord try dis thing on Abraham?" Jasper asked in a singularly cool manner. "I tell yer why. Gord not only wants ter know His people iz all rite, but He wants de wurl' ter know dat dey iz all rite, an' more dan dat, He wants His people ter hev de comfut dat dey is all rite too. Over in de Hebrews, most near de en' uv de Bibul, we iz inform'd dat by faith Aberham, wen he wuz tried, offur'd up Isuk. God know'd dat Aberham lov' Isuk better dan anything on de earth, an' dat he got mity big hopes 'bout his son's futur. So de Lord broke on 'im onexpectid an' order'd 'im ter git out ter Mount Morier an' put his son ter death. It look mity hard an' strange ter

Aberham, but he wuk'd it out. He say ef Gord es gwine ter carry out de plan 'bout Isuk raisin' a gret nashun an' he kill Isuk, den de Lord hav ter rais' 'im up agin, an' so he say I'll do wat de Lord tel me an' ax no questions.

"By de way, yonder dey iz, on de top uv de mountin. Aberham put up thar a big altur an' he done tuk dat wood dat Isuk kerried an' put it under de altur to start de fire. He also got de knife laid out dar shinin' in de sun, sharp es a razer. He call Isuk an' Isuk walk up pert an' willin' an' mity intristid in wat's gwine on, an' wonderrin' whar his father gwine to git an offrin', whar de lam' fer de slaughter wuz. Den Aberham ondress Aisuk an' tie his feet an' han's an' lay 'im up on dat altur. Solem time, I tell yer. Den he turn roun' an' pick up dat blade an' he turn roun' ter de altur an' up he lif' his gret arm high over his hed wid de knife in his han'. It stay up dar a sekkun', an' den wid a suddin flash down it starts.

"Oh, my Gord! Aberham's han' 's parrerlized; fer de earth farly shuk wid de mity vois uv de Lord Gord: 'Aberham, Aberham, hol' on! Lay not thy han' erpon de chile uv de Promis'. I jes' wan' ter try yer!' Wat dat out dar in de brush erblatin' and erscramblin'? Gord had prepar'd de sacrerfice, an' Aberham, undoin' de boy's han's an' feet, hugs 'im ter his hart and cries and shouts tell it look lik de pillers uv de heavens trimbul'd wid de joy."

Now this is the way I remember it, but Jasper was never put on paper. If you were not there, you don't understand. Of course, it was foolish in me, but that great crowd was in such a tumult, and John Jasper seemed in some way so transfigured, and, without knowing why, I was greatly tempted to let out one tremendous yell. There was something in me that needed to be let off, and I cannot tell what I really did, and no matter any way. The strain was so pitiless that I wanted fresh air and would probably have gone out, except that it was the one thing that was physically impossible.

Yet another scene comes back to me. Jasper had paraded his Scriptures in long array in support of his view, that the sun do move, and he had such a tempestuous sense of victory that he turned loose all of his legions upon his scientific antagonists. He called them his "Ferloserfers" and talked hotly about the books which they were all the time sending him. He said that he would like to "huddle all dese books in a pile an' cornsine 'em ter de flames. Dat's wat ought ter be done. Dey ar weppuns wid wich Satun wud 'stroy de Word uv Gord."

The approval of this radical proceeding was accentuated with groans, and shouts, and scornful laughter, which surged through the house like a maddened river. As a fact, I am not much ahead of Jasper in scientific knowledge, but I am not one of those flabby sort who jumped up to say that Jasper was simply voicing what they had believed all the time. Through it all, I kept on believing in the rotation of the earth, just as I had before, and I really thought before I got there that I would get enough fun out of the occasion to supply me for scores of Sundays. The curious result of it all was that Jasper didn't convert me to his theory, nor did he convert me to his religion, but he did convert me to himself. I found myself turning to him with a respect and kindliness of feeling that greatly surprised me. I felt his greatness. I believed in his sincerity, and to me he was a philosopher, sound in his logic, mighty in his convictions, though he might be wrong in his premises.

Now in plain contradiction of what I have said I must make an admission. In the triumph of his ending Jasper polled his crowd to see how his theory was prospering. He bade everybody who really endorsed his theory that the sun moved to show the hand. I stretched up my arm about four feet, and would have punched the ceiling with my fingers if it could have been done. Yes, I voted that the earth was flat and had four corners, and that the sun drove his steeds from the gates of the morning over to the barns in the West, and I never asked the question for a moment as to how the team was got back during the night. Call me a hypocrite, if it will comfort you to do it; that's a very gentle way to speak to a reporter, but I was dead sincere. My vote was in favour of Jasper's logic, his genuineness, his originality, his philosophic honesty, and his religion. If it was hypocrisy to hold up the hand on that occasion, then there was a mammoth pile of hypocrites; for it seemed to me that there were forty hundred of the Brirareus family present and that the last one of them tried to hold up each one of his hands higher than all of his other hands and higher than anybody else's hands.

I got full wages for my vote. To look at old Jasper with his parted lips, his smile, which belied every sign of his oratorical ferocity and vengefulness, and his unspeakable aspect of conquest and glory as the people wrung his hand and poured their happy benedictions upon him.

After the sermon the old brother, with the snow-capped head and the shaking voice, struck up one of the prayer-meeting choral songs. He spun it out rather thin, but reinforcements came in, and by the time they struck the chorus the tramp of the feet all in unison seemed to me strong enough to crash down the bridge over Niagara, and as for the singing, its appeal was to the imagination,--at least to mine,--and I actually fancied that I could hear the invisible choirs in which armies of angels and nations of the ransomed were joining with full voice.

I had Jasper for breakfast, dinner, and supper that week. Down at the office they called me "Jasper," and up at the boarding-house the landlady's boy, who stayed in bed next day from his bruises, was constantly singing, and making me help him, the choral song with which the meeting broke up and the old Yankee preacher and the inevitable boy had me telling all the time of the multitudinous things that happened at Jasper's church.

Months and months have since gone. The Jasperian uproar has ebbed, and I am still the bad reporter, and latterly have changed my desk and work on Sunday, but often and often I dream about Jasper, and every time I dream I fancy that I have joined his church and that he and I shouted when he baptized me. No, I have never been back. I do not wish to build on to my experience, and I do not want it marred by finding Jasper less commanding and kinglike than he was on that spring time Sabbath that afternoon of '78.

XV
JASPER'S PICTURE OF HEAVEN

I NEVER heard Jasper preach a sermon on heaven, nor did I ever hear of his doing so. So far as my observation goes, sermons on heaven have failed to edify the thoughtful--sometimes proving distinctly disappointing. It was not to Jasper's taste to argue on heaven as a doctrine. With him it was as if he were camping outside of a beautiful city, knowing much of its history and inhabitants, and in joyous expectation of soon moving into it. The immediate things of the kingdom chiefly occupied his attention; but when his sermons took him into the neighbourhood of heaven, he took fire at once and the glory of the celestial city lit his face and cheered his soul. This chapter deals only with one of his sermons which, while not on heaven, reveals his heart-belief in it, and its vital effect upon his character.

Imagine a Sunday afternoon at his church--a fair, inspiring day. His house was thronged to overflowing. It was the funeral of two persons-- William Ellyson and Mary Barnes. The text is forgotten, but the sermon is vividly recalled.

From the start Jasper showed a burden and a boldness that promised rich things for his people. At the beginning he betrayed some hesitation--unusual for him. "Lemme say," he said, "a word about dis William Ellersin. I say it de fust an' git it orf mer min'. William

Ellersin was no good man--he didn't say he wus; he didn't try to be good, an' de tell me he die as he live, 'out Gord an' 'out hope in de worl'. It's a bad tale to tell on 'im, but he fix de story hissef. As de tree falls dar mus it lay. Ef you wants folks who live wrong to be preached and sung to glory, don' bring 'em to Jasper. Gord comfut de monur and warn de onruly.

"But, my bruthrin," he brightened as he spoke, "Mary Barnes wus difrunt. She wer wash'd in de blood of de Lam' and walk'd in white; her r'ligion was of Gord. Yer could trust Mary anywhar; nuvr cotch 'er in dem playhouses ner friskin' in dem dances; she wan' no street-walk'r trapsin' roun' at night. She love de house of de Lord; her feet clung to de straight and narrer path; I know'd her. I seen her at de prarmeetin'--seed her at de supper--seed her at de preachin', an' seed her tendin' de sick an' helpin' de mounin' sinn'rs. Our Sister Mary, good-bye. Yer race is run, but yer crown is shure."

From this Jasper shot quite apart. He was full of fire, humour gleamed in his eye, and freedom was the bread of his soul. By degrees he approached the realm of death, and he went as an invader. A note of defiant challenge rang in his voice and almost blazed on his lips. He escorted the Christian to the court of death, and demanded of the monster king to exhibit his power to hurt. It was wonderful to see how he pictured the high courage of the child of God, marching up to the very face of the king of terrors and demanding that he come forth and do his worst. Death, on the other hand, was subdued, slow of speech, admitted his defeat, and proclaimed his readiness to serve the children of Immanuel. Then he affected to put his mouth to the grave and cried aloud: "Grave! Grave! Er Grave!" he cried as if addressing a real person, "Whar's yer vict'ry? I hur you got a mighty banner down dar, an' you turrurizes ev'rybody wat comes long dis way. Bring out your armies an' furl fo'th your bann'rs of vict'ry. Show your han' an' let 'em see wat you kin do." Then he made the grave reply: "Ain't got no vict'ry now; had vict'ry, but King Jesus pars'd through dis country an' tord my banners down. He says His peopl' shan't be troubled no mo' forev'r; an' He tell me ter op'n de gates an' let 'um pass on dar way to glory."

"Oh, my Gord," Jasper exclaimed in thrilling voice, "did yer hur dat? My Master Jesus done jerk'd de sting of death, done broke de scept'r of de king of tur'rs, an' He dun gone inter de grave an' rob it uv its victorous banners, an' fix'd nice an' smooth for His people ter pass through. Mo' en dat, He has writ a song, a shoutin' anthim for us to sing when we go thur, passin' suns an' stars, an' singin' dat song, 'Thanks be onter Gord--be onter Gord who give us de vict'ry thru de Lord Jesus Christ.'" Too well I know that I do scant justice to the greatness of Jasper by this outline of his transcendent eloquence. The whole scene, distinct in every detail, was before the audience, and his responsive hearers were stirred into uncontrollable excitement.

"My bruthrin," Jasper resumed very soberly, "I oft'n ax myself how I'd behave merself ef I was ter git to heav'n. I tell you I would tremble fo' de consequinces. Eben now when I gits er glimpse--jist a peep into de palis of de King, it farly runs me ravin' 'stracted. What will I do ef I gits thar? I 'spec I'll make er fool of myself, 'cause I ain't got de pritty ways an' nice manners my ole Mars' Sam Hargrove used to have, but ef I git thar they ain't goin' to put me out. Mars' Sam'll speak fur me an' tell 'em to teach me how to do. I sometimes thinks if I's 'lowed to go free--I 'specs to be free dar, I tell you, b'leve I'll jest do de town--walkin' an' runnin' all roun' to see de home which Jesus dun built for His people.

"Fust of all, I'd go down an' see de river of life. I lov's to go down to de ole muddy Jemes--mighty red an' muddy, but it goes 'long so gran' an' quiet like 'twas 'tendin' to ' business--but dat ain't nothin' to the river which flows by de throne. I longs fer its chrystal waves, an' de trees on de banks, an' de all mann'rs of fruits. Dis old head of mine oft'n gits hot with fever, aches all night an' rolls on de piller, an' I has many times desired to cool it in that blessed stream as it kisses de banks of dat upper Canaan. Bl'ssed be de Lord! De thought of seein' dat river, drinkin' its water an' restin' un'r dose trees--" Then suddenly Jasper began to intone a chorus in a most affecting way, no part of which I can recall except the last line: "Oh, what mus' it be to be thar?" "Aft'r dat," Jasper continued with quickened note, I'd turn out an' view de beauties of de city--de home of my Father. I'd stroll up dem abenuse whar de children of Gord dwell an' view dar mansions. Father Abraham, I'm sure he got a grate pallis, an' Moses, what 'scorted de children of Israel out of bondige thru' de wilderness an' to de aidge of de promised lan', he must be pow'rful set up being sich er man as he is; an' David, de king dat made pritty songs, I'd like to see 'is home, an' Paul, de mighty scholar who got struck down out in de 'Mascus road, I want to see his mansion, an' all of 'em. Den I would cut roun' to de back streets an' look for de little home whar my Saviour set my mother up to housekeepin' when she got thar. I 'spec to know de house by de roses in de yard an' de vine on de poch." As Jasper was moving at feeling pace along the path of his thoughts, he stopped and cried: "Look dar; mighty sweet house, ain't it lovely?" Suddenly he sprang back and began to shout with joyous clapping of hands. "Look dar; see dat on de do; hallelujah, it's John Jasper. Said He was gwine to prepar a place for me; dar it is. Too good for a po' sinner like me, but He built it for me, a turn-key job, an' mine forev'r." Instantly he was singing his mellow chorus ending as before with: "Oh, what mus' it be to be thar!"

From that scene, he moved off to see the angelic host. There were the white plains of the heavenly Canaan--a vast army of angels with their bands of music, their different ranks and grades, their worship before the throne and their pealing shouts as they broke around the throne of God. The charm of the scene was irresistible; it lifted everybody to a sight of heaven, and it was all real to Jasper. He seemed entranced. As the picture began to fade up rose his inimitable chorus, closing as always: "Oh, what mus' it be to be thar!"

Then there was a long wait. But for the subdued and unworldly air of the old preacher--full seventy years old then--the delay would have dissolved the spell. "An' now, frenz," he said, still panting and seeking to be calm, "ef yer'll 'scuse me, I'll take er trip to de throne an' see de King in 'is roy'l garmints." It was an event to study him at this point. His earnestness and reverence passed all speech, and grew as he went. The light from the throne dazzled him from afar. There was the great white throne-- there, the elders bowing in adoring wonder--there, the archangels waiting in silence for the commands of the King--there the King in His resplendent glory--there in hosts innumerable were the ransomed. In point of vivid description it surpassed all I had heard or read. By this time the old negro orator seemed glorified. Earth could hardly hold him. He sprang about the platform with a boy's alertness; he was unconsciously waving his handkerchief as if greeting a conqueror; his face was streaming with tears; he was bowing before the Redeemer; he was clapping his hands, laughing, shouting and wiping the blinding tears out of his eyes. It was a moment of transport and unmatched wonder to every one, and I felt as if it could never cease, when suddenly in a new note he broke into his chorus, ending with the soul-melting words: "Oh, what mus' it be to be thar!"

It was a climax of climaxes. I supposed nothing else could follow. We had been up so often and so high we could not be carried up again. But there stood Jasper, fully seeing the situation. He had seen it in advance and was ready. "My bruthrin," said he as if in apology, "I dun fergot somethin'. I got ter tek anuth'r trip. I ain't visit'd de ransum of de Lord. I can't slight dem. I knows heap ov 'em, an' I'm boun' to see 'em." In a moment he had us out on the celestial plains with the saints in line. There they were--countless and glorious! We walked the whole line and had a sort of universal handshake in which no note of time was taken. "Here's Brer Abul, de fust man whar got here; here's Brer Enoch whar took er stroll and straggled inter glory; here's ole Ligie, whar had er carriage sent fur 'im an' comed a nigher way to de city." Thus he went on greeting patriarchs, prophets, apostles, martyrs, his brethren and loved ones gone before until suddenly he sprang back and raised a shout that fairly shook the roof. "Here she is; I know'd sh'd git here; why, Mary Barnes, you got home, did yer?" A great handshake he gave her and for a moment it looked as if the newly-glorified Mary Barnes was the centre of Jasper's thoughts; but, as if by magic, things again changed and he was singing at the top of his voice the chorus which died away amid the shrieks and shouts of his crowd with his plaintive note: "Oh, what mus' it be to be thar!"

Jasper dropped exhausted into a chair and some chief singer of the old-time sort, in noble scorn of all choirs, struck that wondrous old song, "When Death Shall Shake

My Frame," and in a moment the great building throbbed and trembled with the mighty old melody. It was sung only as Jasper's race can sing, and especially as only Jasper's emotional and impassioned church could sing it. This was Jasper's greatest sermon. In length it was not short of an hour and a half--maybe it was longer than that. He lifted things far above all thought of time, and not one sign of impatience was seen. The above sketch is all unworthy of the man or the sermon. As for the venerable old orator himself he was in his loftiest mood--free in soul, alert as a boy, his imagination rioting, his action far outwent his words, and his pictures of celestial scenes glowed with unworldly lustre. He was in heaven that day, and took us around in his excursion wagon, and turning on the lights showed us the City of the Glorified.

What is reported here very dimly hints at what he made us see. Not a few of Richmond's most thoughtful people, though some of them laid no claim to piety, were present and not one of them escaped the profound spiritual eloquence of this simple-hearted old soldier of the cross.

Valiant, heroic old man! He stood in his place and was not afraid. He gave his message in no uncertain words--scourged error wherever it exposed its front stood sentinel over the word of God and was never caught sleeping at his post.

When his work ended, he was ready to go up and see his Master face to face.

The stern old orator, brave as a lion, rich in humour, grim, and a dreamer whose dreams were full of heaven, has uttered his last message and gone within the veil to see the wonders of the unseen. If the grapes of Eschol were so luscious to him here, "Oh, what must it be for him to be there."

JOHN JASPER

www.ingramcontent.com/pod-product-compliance
Lightning Source LLC
Chambersburg PA
CBHW081408270326
41931CB00016B/3411